Ecstasy

DISSEMINATIONS
Psychoanalysis In Contexts

Series Editor: Anthony Molino

Reason and Unreason:
Psychoanalysis, Science and Politics
by Michael Rustin

Where Id Was:
Challenging Normalization in Psychoanalysis
edited by Anthony Molino and Christine Ware

Dreams and Drama:
Art and Psychoanalytic Criticism
by Alan Roland

Culture, Subject, Psyche:
Anthropology, Social Theory and Psychoanalysis
by Anthony Molino and Wesley Shumar

The Vitality of Objects:
Exploring the Work of Christopher Bollas
edited by Joseph Scalia

Ecstasy

Michael Eigen

WESLEYAN UNIVERSITY PRESS Middletown, Connecticut

Published by Wesleyan University Press,
Middletown, CT 06459

Set in Carter Cone Galliard
by Keystone Typesetting, Inc.
Manufactured in the United States of America

ISBN 0-8195-6530-X (cloth)
ISBN 0-8195-6531-8 (pbk.)
Cataloging data for this book is available from
the Library of Congress.

5   4   3   2   1

CONTENTS

"Ecstasy is the heart's center." So the book begins. If this statement is true, then it applies to the human heart everywhere. Years ago I heard Hanna Arendt speak about the secret ecstasy in intellectual work. She said that she felt a little embarrassed using a term usually reserved for mystics, lovers, or poets. But, above all, she confessed, it is ecstasy that drives the love of thinking.

I wrote this book in response to an inner pressure to express the ecstasy underlying psychoanalytic work, as well as life more generally—an ecstasy coming through, often wedded with, the most excruciating states. In *The Electrified Tightrope* (1993), I called attention to the profound joy that is to be found in working through psychoanalytic agonies. Often this joy is defended against by analyst and patient alike, an evasion buttressed by overly narrow ideas of what psychoanalysis is or ought to be. In *Ecstasy*, I portray the psychoanalytic heart beating through a range of experiences significant for who we are; pleasures and pains—threatening to sink the soul—culminate in faith and openness.

Somewhat later, in *The Psychoanalytic Mystic* (1998), I portrayed an originary, boundless *jouissance* funneled through analytic desire. In one form or another, this *jouissance* may be part of every psychic act, part of the medium or field that personality lives, breathes, grows in. It connects with Federn's originary, boundless I-feeling, Winnicott's going on being, Milner's orgasmic core of symbolic experiencing, Bion's Faith. One may narcissistically appropriate and exploit this *jouissance*. But one may, too, become aware of its challenge and begin the intricate journey of serving *jouissance* everywhere, in the other as well as in the self.

This book argues for an ecstatic core to psychoanalysis and life in general. It's "argument" is less rationalistic and linear, more a moment-to-moment showing of creative and destructive ecstasies at work. In the pages ahead, I draw heavily on psychotherapy sessions and psychoanalytic thinking, but also touch aspects of mystical experiencing from antiquity to the present. Psychoanalysis and mystical experiencing illuminate and transform each other, flourish beyond denominational lines. I hope my book is a kind of dance, perhaps a kind of psychoanalytic poetry.

A light at the center of personality must face and come through conditions threatening the very basis of its being. *Ecstasy* focuses on the ever necessary confrontation of a mystical core with suffering, degradation, annihilation, and an endless play of destructive forces that exert deforming pressures. It is an affirmation of the faith journey through psychoanalysis and contemporary life made more intense by relentless pursuit of catastrophes of self. The book's momentum gathers diverse psychoanalytic schools and includes blends and reworkings of Freud, Lewin, Lacan, Bion, Winnicott, Jung, Reich, and Kohut, rubbing against, sometimes melding with, Plato, Plotinus, William Blake, the Bible, Shakespeare, Kabbala, Spielberg, and everyday dramas of corruption and integrity.

One person's ecstasy may be another person's horror. There are destructive as well as creative ecstasies, ecstasies of war and injury, brutal ecstasies. Plato critiqued poetic intoxication and delusional aspects of sensory-emotional rapture, even if an ecstatic current infuses Socrates' Vision of the Good. Ecstasies of pain and trauma confuse soul and mind. In light of miseries wrought by ecstatic destruction, no critique of ecstasy can be too strong. History is filled with stunning abuse between groups and persons fueled by ecstatic processes that sour, take cruel ideological turns, pit being against being. Ecstasy and its twin, ecstasy envy, readily meld into a righteous rage that can be all too calculating.

Nevertheless, I believe an underlying ecstasy helps us feel real, adds to life's color, fuels vision, and is part of the tone and texture of our lives. It is not a matter of whether we can or cannot live with or without it. It is a capacity we must pay attention to, study as well as enjoy, and learn to learn from. We cannot get rid of it, anymore than we can rid ourselves of breathing. But we may be able to evolve with it, as we become better partners with the capacities that constitute us.

In the past I wrote of madness (1986), deadness (1996), and damage

(1999, 2001) and, at times, noted radiance following lines of trauma. In *Ecstasy*, this radiance, the Light that lifts and shatters, is center stage. Every attempt to grapple with a capacity as truly as one can adds to the feel of what is possible. My prayer is that my work joins this groping, this struggle to learn how to be, a journey ever opening.

Ecstasy

Ecstasy is the heart's center. The heart of life. It is not reserved for the soul's union with God, although that is where it starts and ends. It pervades the body, the inside and outside of skin, the pulsing of organs. It is in the senses, touching, hearing, seeing. It is in the body's movements, muscles, mucous membranes, flow of breath and blood. In the Bible, Israel is told not to eat the blood of animals because the soul is in the blood. Ecstasy is in the blood.

Blood ecstasies can be terrible. Not just ecstasies of sex, but ecstasies of murder, ecstasies of fear and rage. There are patients who must cut themselves, see and smear and taste their blood, not only to feel real but to feel ecstatic. There are individuals who must cut others to tap a stream of ecstasy.

The blood-soul-ecstasy bond is ancient. One senses it in cave paintings between hunter and hunted, exquisite, tantalizing, breathtaking beauty of the hunt. Death-life feed each other, soul of the hunt. Twist the sense of power and you have the frenzy of Nazi calculation, chills of exaltation and stupor, extermination ecstasies. You have blood-soul cementing the United States in civil war, the War between the States — states of mind as well as political-economic geography.

Seal a contract with blood-soul. God with Abraham: every sexual sensation is a reminder of God. Yes, God is in the soul of the blood, the pulsations. God of sex and murder. God of ecstasy. God beyond ecstasy. D. H. Lawrence's sexual god of the blood. Night gods seeping into day.

One does not have to maim or kill to find ecstasy. Pascal's famous cup of coffee triggered outpourings of the God of Fire. Not vision so much as upwelling of feeling, transfiguring rapture. God of Abraham, Isaac, and Jacob, espresso genie, lighting the night. All the Hindus, Buddhists, sitting, sitting, sitting. Stillness ecstasies. One needn't lift a finger, scarcely need breathe.

A group of students talked about God all night, then all day, then all night again. Months passed. Years. Some of these students never made a living. Books and thought and meditation were all. In time, talk and thought faded. They sat all day and night and felt God. They found the ecstasy center. They drew themselves around it. The flame glistened and glowed. There was nothing else. Some of these students starved to death. They became the ecstasy center, nothing else. Some became poets, scientists, businessmen. Some remained students and survived in precarious ways.

Human spirit feeds on tiger soul: "Tiger, tiger burning bright." Predator God becomes spiritual prey. We eat God as God devours us. Spiritual cannibals, we take power and virtue from each other. All kinds of spirits in a person touch us. We take in each other's spirits, pick the bones of this trait or ability.

What do mothers do for babies? Provide feelings, like air, for baby's feeling self. A baby lives in a feeling atmosphere. A smile, a touch, endless streams of feelings. Everything visible is invisible: the baby abides in worlds of infinite invisibility, invisible feelings. A mother's face can be the visible infinite.

Some babies turn into tigers.

When a tiger reaches old age, soul claps hands and sings.

Freud's work is a song to ecstasy, at once ecstatic and anti-ecstatic.

In the beginning, chaotic sensory streams, pleasure streams, unlocalizeable pain points. In the beginning, a pleasure I, I filled with pleasure, wanting only pleasure. Pleasure always — as Pascal hoped the moment of Fire would never fade. In the beginning, a narcissistic I unifying (in some fashion) sensory streaming. Pleasure I shutting out pain. I-feeling trying to identify only with feeling good, well-being, pleasure, bliss, joy, ecstasy.

A growing capacity to hallucinate pleasure, to hallucinate wholeness. Freud's hallucinogenic fantasy, imaginative vision: baby hallucinates breast when breast is missing, hallucinates satisfaction where there is pain.

Great God I — becoming the center of sensory streaming (I sense, I feel, I think) — tries to legislate pain out of existence, place pain outside

I, let pain disappear in outer space. Double movement: (1) *I* spreads and appropriates; (2) *I* consolidates desired territory (pleasure) and sheds bad (pain). Sensation happens, happens to me: *I* sense. Feeling happens, happens to me: *I* feel. Thoughts happen, happen to me: *I* think. A psychic magnifying machine magnifies *I* and its contents.

Hallucination as a first cognition, wish as reality, pleasure over pain — how does this work? *I* scans memory for happy times, remembers good feed, magnifies the picture, replaces bad time now with good time then, now forever. I-it is determined that life feels good, feeling is being. Hungry baby hallucinates good feed, a desert soul seeing water. A good memory, infinitized, substitutes for present difficulty, becomes all that is now, an eraser now, a pain eraser. A present that obliterates the present.

A good feed becomes a perfect feed, a beatific moment. The psychic magnifier-infinitizer translates good to heavenly. Baby learns to make itself happy for a while. All-heavenly cannot be sustained indefinitely, and divine drops into demonic.

How do we develop antihallucinogenic capacities, perceive reality beyond wishes, undertake to face present difficulties? We do so, partly, by making room for pain.

Problem: ecstasy is not pleasure magnified, nor is hell merely pain magnified. A baby growing in a field of ecstasy and hell (including ecstatic hell and hellish ecstasy) is not simply a baby growing in fields of pleasure-pain.

Everyone is a specialist. One lives out a few of many possibilities of self. However many-sided a person is, one is always less than what one "might" have been. One is never all-sided. One = All is an important moment. Such moments leave residues lasting a lifetime. One is All supports life in the background. But lack is crucial for living. Lack provides some protection against utopianism, if not much.

If Wilhelm Reich literalizes the psyche, at least for him life energy and body are real. Sensory streaming quickens life, and we armor ourselves against the stream of life. There are ways in which character is akin to a tight muscle, a shield against sensory flow. Character is armor. Character armor ↔ Body armor. We could not live if we were not shields against life, if we were not shields against ourselves. We cannot live without tightening our characters, tightening our bodies, squeezing ourselves.

Reich places a lot on orgasm. So much self-tightening defends against orgasm. We tighten in the face of intensity. Armor vs. orgasm. Meanness is inadequate orgasm. Orgasmic fulfillment makes us nicer. And if we were nicer, we might open to more orgasmic fulfillment. The schizophrenic and Nazi share orgasmic inadequacy. They seek alternate orgasms: madness and murder. Mysticism is a kind of orgasm. Character is hostility. Orgasm is love. Orgasmic opening subverts lack.

I don't think body is up to such responsibility, but to search for an ethics of the body or place ethics *in* the body makes sense. Ethics and orgasm, body ethics, soul orgasm: variable space-time-infinity combinations.

Nevertheless, lack persists. Some search for perfect orgasm, some for perfect lack. Ought one expect orgasm to cure lack as food cures hunger? Hunger is renewable. Orgasm recurs. There may be parallels but no identity between orgasmic capacity and a good meal.

A good dream sometimes does more than both.

Prophets talk of opening one's heart rather than of genital orgasms. They seem to take the latter for granted. They seem to feel opening one's heart is a kind of orgasm or has orgasmic properties. Orgasm is part of opening one's heart.

Moralists may say orgasm is a by-product of heart's opening, a secondary reward. Opening itself is more important than the orgasmic element. Opening for its own sake is reward enough. Ethical opening, circumcision of the heart. The sacrifice that counts is not animal—but self-giving, opening to the Other, the poor, the widow, the lacking one. One opens to the lack in the Other. Justice and mercy are compassionate responses to lack.

Orgasm can be misleading. Power orgasms, billionaire orgasms, getting rich orgasms. Idolatry orgasms. God orgasms. Ambition orgasms. Ecstasy for one is cruelty for another. What would it be like for a whole society to enjoy an analogue to simultaneous orgasm, no one left out? No one left out — such a strange, unnatural idea. No one left out — God message for our time.

Have there ever been more rich people in the world than there are today? Are there more rich people in the United States today than there have ever been in the world at one time? Have the poor ever been better off? Is the ship rising? I put quarters and dollar bills into the hands of the poor on the street, rather than pennies, nickels, and dimes. They no longer say "thank you" for less.

The ego is the id's first love object, and the ego is its own ideal. What an amazing ego or I. Pumped up from the beginning. No wonder Paul Federn picked up on these Freudian threads and saw the early ego as a cosmic I, boundless. Streams of erotic energy feeding I-feeling. I-feeling feeling ideal. Is everything a comedown after this? The radiant I, pulsating, sun-like, ecstatic in its own existence. Freud tells us the early I's boundaries are coextensive with all that is. One = All.

One is not surprised to learn that primal, ecstatic, boundless I is on a collision course with the facts of life. Boundless I-feeling contracts in the face of pain. A smaller I forms to negotiate limits. Cosmic I and practical I: what will these twins do together throughout a lifetime?

So much emphasis on I. So much going on at once. Freud's work teems with so many currents: blending, warring, uniting, separating, mixing every which way. External World impinges on autistic self-states, on I or self as egg or a self-contained system of energy. The egg is cracked not simply by internal forces pushing out, but also by external impingements pressing in, externality itself, life outside the closed system. There is always life outside a closed system. How many crushing meteors does it take to realize the system isn't entirely closed, even if it isn't entirely open?

How does I-feeling extend to encompass You-feeling?

The I becomes aware of a gap between you and me because there *is* a gap between you and me. If one is hungry and lacks a breast, one can hallucinate a feed only so long. Sooner or later, one must admit a not-me component.

One may scream and mother may come. At times, not fast enough. Time separates self-other. Once the nipple is in and the milk flows, a sense of wholeness comes back, oneness again, but not the same, not totally. Over time, one appreciates the return of the Other, the one who completes me, who fills me, who is part of me but not me.

The sense of wholeness or completion now covers or includes a *not*, a lack. A moment ago *not* was here—no milk, no mother, no completer, no fulfiller. Now there is All again, yumminess, peacefulness, the Good. You are this All for me. You are It for me.

I-radiance, You-radiance: competing-complementary radiances.

I-ecstasies, You-ecstasies: rings or ripples within-outside each other.

Everything gets turned upside down over time. In an ancient view, our unconscious is made up of occluded memories of God, the One, the All, and processes of descent. We tend to forget our origins. Our trek through the unconscious is a movement toward God.

What we have forgotten is not *sub* but *supra*. The over-world, over-soul, the All-Soul. We tend to lose contact with the Higher, saturated by Lower. Filled with our ambition, passion, desire, survival care, weakness—God fades from view. The equipment God gave us to contact Him sinks into unconsciousness and is poorly used or misused.

In an ancient scheme, God is mediated through intellect. There are levels of intellect belonging to God alone, or just below God and just above us, and various levels in us bearing God's imprint, enabling reasoning. Even so, God is not intellect, since the latter presupposes differentiation, even if knower-known are one.

No need for God to think. God is beyond thinking, beyond differentiation and limitation. Yet intellect and reasoning provide something of a ladder to the Beyond.

God's intellect, then, is something of a misnomer. But it is associated with a divine plan, providence, self-sufficiency, self-completion. We get a taste of God through our higher function, a meeting of minds. Yet our higher function is mostly unconscious. We make little use of it. We are more given to lower functions. Little by little, we may be able to animate our reason and begin the ascent. Our intellect may make contact with God's intellect, taste the universal plan, or, more accurately, get a glimpse of the reason the intellect below God plants in us, the reason or intellect our nature allows us to see and use.

The recovery and exercise of Reason jumpstarts the process but does not take us all the way. In the end, what can be known cannot be God, since God, being One, is beyond knowing, which involves duality. It is, finally, a certain ecstasy that brings us to God. We do not know how this happens. We feel our way into it and use suggestive words like "sinking" into God, "merging," being "filled" with God — filled with God, rather than saturated with forgetting. In such moments we forget world, life, lesser passions, ambitions. In such moments there is only God. We turn the unconscious inside out and reach the Fathomless.

But unconsciousness begins again, replete with passions and drives and lost worlds, higher-lower.

How do we get to God through Ecstasy?
"Cut away everything," says Plotinus.

By cutting away everything, Plotinus continues, we discover we are not cut off: "We have not been cut away; we are not separate." We sing our lives, "a choral song full of God."

Plotinus tells us God is ever unchanging rest, repose, and that we rest in God. Rest in peace, we say. Freud associated Nirvana with death.

To us restless ones, ever cutting ourselves away — Rest?

Are "cutters" who cut bodies instead of souls on the wrong track? Their blades want something that can't be touched by metal. Do they feel something ineffable for a moment when they see blood? The soul is in the blood? Or perhaps they angrily insist body is a gateway to ecstasy, the bloody body. No body, no ecstasy.

Cutters are very stubborn. They stick their body in your face to show you it is real. No leaving it behind, as Plotinus does. They cut themselves to remember body, as Plotinus cuts self to remember God. They show you their bloody shame, marks you can't forget. They show you their bloody dread. They cut themselves to prove they are not bloodless, to prove God is not bloodless. They have gone through bloodcurdling experiences, but their blood is still warm. Must we shed blood to prove we are not bloodless, to make life warm?

Blood freezes and curdles. We want it warm and flowing again. We cut ourselves and each other to gain a moment's peace. We cut away everything to reach a God point. God of Rest, God of Fire. Between-beyond Plotinus-Pascal. Bloody gods, bloody bodies.

Plotinus centers thought around a very real core. We can find the point of rest, the Sabbath point of the soul. We can live in God — all good, "soul's peace, outside of evil, refuge taken in the one place clean of wrong."

We do this through our higher soul, a higher principle. Then cut that away too. Not only vices, but also virtues fall away. Naked soul to naked soul. Until soul, too, is superfluous.

We can bring the point of rest into daily cares. It can make lives better.

Too often, trying to bring the point of rest into our lives ignites rages. How many meditators and prayers I've worked with who are ragers! God help those who break into stillness, who disturb peace! Once having tasted peace at the center of being, we find that loved ones are disturbances. Irritants magnify. Kids, mate, co-workers — the contrast between God's peace and actual people seems unbridgeable. Too often, hunger for peace increases violence.

The forming images at the heart of religions are violent. There is a violent core of imagery in the Prince of Peace. Jesus comes with a spiritual sword and is killed in body. Peace in heaven perhaps, not on earth. On earth, agony. The dying-rising God-man: let life be where death is. Freud's hallucinatory element: let triumph substitute for defeat, milk for emptiness, good for evil, peace for pain.

Moses' law links with God's rage, wipes out many. People betray the law, lack faith. They cannot bear the yoke. They lack equipment, ability, will, desire. Still, something in them does have faith, a remnant, a mustard seed. There is desire for God, law, grace, humanity. God is in the melted calf, the anguished bull.

There are aspects of Plotinus's thought with fascist possibilities. If there is love for the Higher, what happens to the Lower? Love for the Beautiful, what of the Ugly? Love of the Healthy, what of the Ill?

The message of the Prophets has another ring. It moves toward the left out (the "left"), the squashed, the victims, the injured, the weak, the ill, the traumatized.

The ultimate Platonic vision is love of the Good — Vision of the Good. Prophetic goodness includes the excluded, the powerless. Envision Plotinus, like Muhammad Ali, hugging an emaciated, puss-oozing child. Can the God of Repose hug a child abused by life? Prophetic goodness sticks bodies in your face, bloody bodies. Prophetic goodness sticks aloneness, death, suffering in your face. Prophetic goodness puts joy in your heart, surrounded by bitterness.

The outcome ought to be compassion. Yet righteous rage abounds. Rage — a loose wire — who knows at who it aims next? Cupid's arrows smite with love. There ought to be a similar image for rage.

Have I done Plotinus an injustice? He doesn't mean physical beauty or ugliness. A beautiful body can house an ugly soul, an ugly body a beautiful soul. He means intellectual beauty, beauty of mind. The intellect, gateway to God, mediates beauty.

Intellect = higher. Sensations, feelings, imaginings = lower. Above-below. Ruling-ruled. The hierarchy easily translates into terms not meant by Plotinus. Those who have–those who have not. Best-worst. Educated-uneducated. Famous-unknown. Celebrated-celebrators. Rich-poor. Successful-unsuccessful.

The Song of Songs tells us God is found in sex. We didn't need the Song of Songs to tell us that. But it does so beautifully.

The Prophets tell us God is found in opening our hearts to the poor, the needy, the underside, the lower. Not only opening, actually aiding, doing, lending helping hands. The graceless term "handout" carries the cynical prejudice of the higher, contempt from on high.

Never lose Plotinus's ecstasy of rest, intellectual ecstasy. Plotinus adds to human possibilities. Why take away from them? Why subtract in order to add?

One can find God in the heart-mind connection, in the heart-hand connection, in the heart-genital connection. We search for the human. Why so much denigration?

Psychoanalysis is a voice for the excluded. It investigates what's left out of the "official" self. Dream-work. Passions. Contradictions, paradoxes, ironies, conflicts.

Psychoanalysis persecutes God for leaving out too much. Psychoanalysis sniffs the ass of higher philosophy. The latter already was falling. Dialectical idealism to dialectical materialism. Freud is a psychical materialist with Platonic elements, a sort of materialistic Platonist. The age of incessant recombinations has begun, the age that creates new elements. Everything mates with everything else. Get used to strange births.

Modernity begins with constructionism. Hobbes tells us the mind knows only what the mind creates. Kant brings out limits of reason against the background of unknowable reality. Whatever we know is mediated by psychophysical apparatuses and operating systems, mind / brain. We learn what we can about our filtering systems, ways we are given to ourselves.

Beyond structure, what about energy? What if psychical systems work with a closed, constant amount of energy? What if the energy is basically sexual? What if sexual energy is envisioned as fluid-electrical, taking endless forms, ceaseless condensations-displacements? What if energy creates structure, and the latter channels and reshapes energy? What about rage — death drive turned outward, or part of life drive, allied with sex? Rage — part of life force, a baby's scream, voice of pain, explosive life?

Platonic white-black horses and charioteer. Id-ego-superego: lower-middle-higher, moving bottom up, bottom repressed-rerouted. Sex everywhere, including God. Sex-rage everywhere, especially God, magnified I, magnified psyche blown up under a microscope. A sexual-raging God everywhere, it-I-superI.

Ancient trinities reworked, holy taken out of them. Reason still there, but not the reason that leads to God. Practical, social, scientific reason — reasoning about conditions of life and psyche and society and matter. An evolutionary reason, evolutionary I. The Golden Mean is there — compromise, balance, working with conflictual tensions. Biblical outrage over hypocrisy is there, coupled with wry observation. What one presents to the world and oneself is a mostly unconscious compromise made up of complex forces, divisions, splits, linkages, possibilities. We used to think we knew something when we saw passions nesting in ideals or saw reason as a whore of power. Now reason itself is an amalgam of elusive processes we know little about.

Cultural traditions do headstands, collapse, become ingredients in shifting collages. "Crises" is an apt term to describe the delirium we call our lives. Some ancients compared life to a dream. We feel dream-work plays a role in structuring life as we know it.

An eye is glued to what is left out. Is this new eye an old eye we notice more, an eye that has grown? An eye on what is left out of the ecstasy of the moment. We are critical of ecstasy because of its exclusions.

Often our eye for what is left out makes us trivial. We bicker with each other over what we don't say. We fight with each other for coming from someplace else. An unconscious feel for sameness reacts against difference. The Other becomes an enemy because of what he or she doesn't include. The Other excludes our sense of sameness. The Other excludes us. One fights to be included but needs to feel excluded (and vice versa).

One needs an enemy, enemy as friend. An enemy provides some illusion of psychic safety by defining danger for a time. Enemies fuel ecstasy. Orgies of hate, revenge, me against you, righteous top dog–bottom dog. The excluded enemy is the included core of warrior-victim ecstasies, bondage ecstasies, sadomasochistic ecstasies. We place the outside we fight against at the center of our rageful beings.

Psychoanalysis says, "What's in this ecstasy?" Psychoanalytic ecstasy says, "I want to see," or maybe, "Let me see you."

"Where are you?" God asks Adam. "Hiding," Adam says, preserving the illusion of being seen and known.

Plotinus oozed puss in his final years, from open sores on his legs and body. People were repulsed. His once-sonorous voice turned raspy and off-putting. He may have had leprosy. Muhammad Ali embraced a child in this condition. Plotinus's last utterance was about uniting with the

Divine. At the moment of his death, a snake slid from under his bed and escaped through a hole in the wall.

A man once consulted me because he feared he would die without finding himself. He had heart disease and had just come out of the hospital in the wake of a heart attack. He was in big trouble at work. He was a counselor in a college and had seduced young men. One of these episodes blew up, and his job was threatened. His most recent heart failure followed. Explosion = explosion.

I became paranoid when he told me he wanted me to write a letter to his college, saying he was in treatment dealing with his problem. I imagined he was hitting on me. He came to see me to get this letter, to keep his job. His rap about finding himself was a cover, a come-on. He would seduce me with the promise of psychoanalysis, the way he seduced young men with the promise of life.

Yet he came. He worked. He dug deeper. He raced time. Psychoanalysis in fast motion. Through layers of history, layers of psyche, the heart and soul of his life and being. Therapy ecstasies, self-knowledge ecstasies replaced ecstasies with young men. There was no time for both in those final months. Fear of losing his job was not the only spur. Time itself was the driving force: now or never.

There were moments when he had a sense of being at rest, perhaps not Plotinus's rest, not divine union, but perhaps not entirely removed from it either. More like Bion's sense of at-onement with self. He felt at peace with himself and his life. For the first time, he felt truly honest, as honest as his "taint" (his word) let him be. It is difficult to say what he meant by "taint," but it includes a disposition to deceive, a twist no amount of honesty can undo. Nevertheless, honesty grows, puts pressure on the twist of self, increasing hunger for truth the more impossible the latter seems to be. Something true comes through the taint, in spite of the latter, and makes contact with the true being of the Other. For the first time, he felt heard, seen, appreciated, accepted, loved — as he was, as much himself as he could be. I felt deeply moved being let in to such intimate chambers. We thanked each other.

One day he reported a dream of a black cat disappearing into a basement window. He died later that day walking into a subway.

A man consults me and says he wants to find himself before he dies. We are the same age. He already has a pacemaker. "I'm a failure," he keeps saying. He lists everything he can that clings to his failed self. He is a failure at work, in marriage, with friends, with himself. He looks like a nice guy, open, full. But he tells me he flies into rages and vanishes. He is not there. He flickers in and out of life through momentary rages, but does not stay long.

"I've connived and schemed my whole life, taking the easy way. I've a winning way. People trust me. I know how to get people to invest in me. But there is a hole, a vacancy. I vanish. I inflate myself. I fill up with self-importance, convince everyone I'm bigger than life. I convince myself. I get so big I disappear, make mistakes, bad judgments, lose everything, as if to prove I'm not what I thought I was. I make and lose fortunes. I get high on myself. I can't stop inflating my worth, ability, accomplishments, then falling. Even now I feel myself bragging, watching my effect on you. I want to rip that away. I want to contact myself. When I make contact with myself, I find nothing."

I feel him playing me. I'm suspicious and think of the joke, "Look who calls himself a nothing." I can see he wants my sympathy and is afraid he'll repulse me. But I also feel he *is* sincere, as much as he can be. He is stuck with himself, can't get out of the trap he is in, and fears he is about to lose a life he never found. I sit paralyzed, dumbfounded, just feeling the impact of his condition, the twists and turns of it, the knot and maze of being.

He is addicted to pumping himself up, an ugly distorted ecstasy, a taste of heaven nonetheless. An ecstasy bubble that always bursts because of the hole in the middle. I believe his sense of failure, his nothing, even if he plays on it. I believe he is determined to say what he sees, even if he can't.

He wants to stay with his nothing and wants me to know from the start he will do everything he can to inflate it. Therapists he had visited tried to help him find *something*. After all, he looks like *someone*. He is coherent, cordial, interactive, someone you want to make feel better, someone you believe is unfairly down on himself. But what if he simply is right? What if *no one* is home?

He lays his cards on the table. Self-inflation pervades everything. He tries to get to nothing as antidote but inflates even this. When he looks at himself, he sees nothing but failure, including failure to be nothing. When he tries to strip nothing of self-inflation, he collapses into agonized seminothing, a dull, glowing misery, tinged with tormented ecstasy. It is the sour ecstasy that lies undigested in depression. "I can't even be nothing right" is his signature.

He has fallen into a lie and can't get out. Whatever direction he moves in, the lie moves with him. He lives inside it. His sense of failure is attached to being a lie. He hopes nothing will cleanse the lie and is horrified that nothing lies too. He can't get rid of himself, can't lose himself to find himself. Self sticks to everything.

"Nothing takes practice," I stammer, trying to feel my way in. "It's hard being nothing. Inflation is easy. Inflation comes naturally." I don't mean to make fun of him but there's a ghastly humor here. I can't help reflecting it. I feel he tells the truth about lying. I can feel him feeling twisted, lame. I can feel his longing to feel right. This is what the Bible is about—the lame will walk, the warped will be whole. There is faith somewhere in the room, in the face of impossibility.

"If we fail to find nothing, everything seems a lie," I sum.

"Everything *is* a lie," he instantaneously retorts. His face is anguished, tears fall.

For the moment, I feel something, an impalpable fact. I feel *him. He* actually spoke. For an instant, he comes through. I feel him feel surprise. A moment's point of contact. An instant's taut peace.

Inside myself I bemoan the fact that words and thoughts are forming. I feel silence is better. But words form: "If you're nothing long and true enough, maybe something you can say yes to will grow." I hate myself for thinking this. How Pollyannaish, corrupt. To say it would spoil everything. In the end, I'm like all therapists, like all parents, wanting something to come of it. In spite of myself, the words push out.

"I'd like that," he says. We look at each other a while. "You're feeling what it's like to be me," he said, after quite some time. "You're feeling me. You're feeling my life."

Instead of quick-hit ecstasies, a moment's pause.

We sat, two nothings. Enjoying a little something.

Bertram Lewin writes of breast as dream screen, dream screen as breast. He describes an "oral triad." The hungry baby has a good feed, feels satisfaction, sleeps. Peaceful feeling transforms into blank background supporting dreams. Fullness = nothingness = everythingness. Blank bliss screen supporting dreams.

Psychoanalysts emphasize frustration — not having mother — as the moment that promotes the growth of symbolization. One creates a symbol where frustration — no mother — is. Instead of literal mother, symbolic mother.

Lewin's breast = dream screen suggests that satisfaction supports symbols. Images are born of bliss, take bliss to new places.

Images express the waxing-waning of ecstasy as well as agony. Images connect intense feelings, one kind or another.

Instead of empty breast, full breast. After the feed — if things go well — the full breast is enshrined in dream life. An ever full breast supports dreams. Full breast, full belly, full body, full heart, full mind. The breast that supports life gives birth to dreaming. Dreams nourish the spirit, feed the psyche, milk for the mind.

What if things don't go well enough? What if they go horribly? What if the dream screen is warped, mutilated? Everything that appears on it will be warped or mutilated. What if the dream screen is a black hole or marked with holes? Dreams cannot be dreamt. They are sucked into the dream screen before they can be born. Or they appear with areas of damage, damaged dreams for damaged psyches.

One of life's cruel tantalizations is that there are black hole ecstasies, mutilated ecstasies, damaged and damaging ecstasies, including evil imaginings, evil dreams. Ecstasy plays in damaged keys. One keeps aiming at the ecstasy in the warp, pressing buttons to heighten it. There is a sense one can undo the warp by feeding on ecstatic twists. Can warp continue after bliss? Warped breast and nipple, warped mouth and tongue, poisoned milk, poisoned mind. In the extreme, monstrous ecstasies.

Good-bad breast-mind. Good-bad infinitized: divine-demonic. Suppose the two commingle or are superimposed on each other? Good tinged by evil, evil by good, filters for experiencing each other. The dream screen varies. Variable feed, variable dreams, more horrible, more wonderful. Juxtapositions-condensations of beatific-mutilated moments. Does the good ecstasy make the twisted ecstasy better? Does warped ecstasy make divine ecstasy worse? Can one be sure what one is made of, what one tastes like, or what the next taste of spirit will be?

And if the two are one?

Lewin notes a dream light, a luminosity. A blank and full dream screen indicator, overflow of good feed-sleep. There is, too, a black hole "screen," or "screenlessness," where the last scream disappears through dread into hopeless stupor. Traumatizing feed or no feed deforms into spectral dread, tortured affect, mutilated affectlessness, ghastly nothing. Divine malignant light, heavenly ghastly darkness. Self simultaneously is hellpurgatoryheaven. Dramas in time distribute distinctions as incessant interplay. Divine light, ghastly agony in and through each other. Nothing without goodnesswarp.

It takes my mother a long time to die. She has a strong heart, strong vital signs. Her brain is being eaten away by microstrokes, a dementia. She can no longer be out of bed, walk, hold herself up. A sickening black sore forms on the bottom of her foot where blood scarcely flows. She no longer can put words together, make sentences. Now and then phrases come. Now and then one of them makes sense.

Seeing her is totally heartwrenching, heartbreaking.

She holds my hand with a strong grip, puts my hand to her mouth. I kiss her cheeks. She gasps with love. I feel her love. God cut her down, whittled away everything except love. Goodness shines through the ruins.

There are moments when I feel her fury, her rage at disability. Her mother told her old age is golden. Her mother died in her forties of breast cancer. My mother's old age is horrible.

Still—the goodness, the glow. Only the essence is left, the very essence. I see God in her face, her heart. Her heart—my heart. I see God, feel God, a golden, luminous center.

"How is your mother?" my wife asks.

"Ghastly," I say. "Ghastly." My heart opens, glow everywhere, sad, wrenching glow, deep, deep radiance.

My mother's mother looked old to me. Wrinkled, thin. I called her "Monkey." I couldn't help it. My mother sometimes seemed a little wounded. She felt for her mother. She knew time meant something.

In those days kids sometimes were called monkeys. Lovingly, I suppose. All these terms so mixed. I hated being called monkey, like being called cute. Adult disparagement. Not to be taken seriously, like one's own self. The discomfort of children a source of amusement, funny pain.

I guess I turned it on my grandma and she took it. Why? Because she was weak? A victim? Years later her look of love came to me. In my twenties, my thirties, I wept and wept. I could feel myself a baby in her arms, her kind face, loving eyes. What was I seeing? Precious, something precious. I felt precious in her arms. God!

When I was a little boy, she somewhat scared me, the wrinkles, the bonyness, like death. I poured it on, blew the fear up, made the most of it, fed her the funny pain, the monkey pain, deflected it from me to her, and she took it. It meant little to her. What was precious—*that* meant a lot, that meant *everything*.

I didn't understand what cancer meant for a long time. She was in bed dying, then came back. She saw beautiful bearded men in prayer shawls. She was happy. Light. Golden glow everywhere. Shining, halos. Beauty, fullness. They gently told her it was not time, she had to go back, she would return soon.

My grandma came back to the living and told us all she had seen and felt. She lived several more years. More time for me to absorb the deep precious feeling, the deep gold, while I called her monkey and loved to see her light candles on Friday nights, mysterious candles.

My mother told me that when she was young she was ashamed of her mother. She dressed in *schmattas*, spoke Yiddish, never learned English — simple woman, old country. My mom was proud of her father — sharp dresser, sharp talker, making the most of America, with deals and pushcarts filled with everything. His broken English made my spine tingle. She would show him off to her girlfriends, while she hid her mother.

My mother told me that as she grew older she came to feel what her mother gave her was more lasting, more important: good heart, good values, plain love, not showy, simple, caring. Mom felt this saw her through, this gave her strength, tied it all together. She appreciated the simple being she felt ashamed of.

Now in my sixties I feel my mother's passed some of it to me. My wife has it, a good heart. Do my kids? Third or fourth generation? Computer-age, postmodern? But they have it. I see it, feel it. I count on it, the precious core, the most important thing. Deep heart's opening. Pass it on and on and on, God be willing.

I ask a twelve year old what he most feels in life. He turns it back and says, "You tell me first." I say, "Agony and ecstasy, pain and joy." He says he thinks there is just agony. Variations of agony. He insists, "Joy is the lowest level of agony."

Many people want the agony to go away. Any agony seems too much. Yet this boy lives with honest agony. Agony as a baseline is manageable. That is what he knows. No one has confused him about it. Life bothers him. Life pains him. He thinks of being a writer. Writers write from never-ending pain.

Writers beat their chests with longing, hoping writing will make them whole. Someone will hear, heal.

Some cannot settle for personal healing. They point to injustice lacerating the social body. They cannot rest if that is not healed as well. There can be no social or personal healing apart from each other.

A mystic says longing is separation from God. Some say matter separates. We unite with God through mind, soul, spirit, intuition. Body is the gap. We unite with God as best we can until shedding our physical barrier, our shell.

We agree with Dostoevsky: a dying child is an evil that lacerates philosophical beauty. Goodness dies when a child dies. Jesus does not only die in body; spirit is crucified too — the human spirit. The human spirit is reduced to agony. Shattered by a final agony, and another final agony, and another. Why do philosophers say such shattering is needed for spiritual transmutation? They're not entirely wrong.

My twelve year old's agony goes on and on. He sees a butterfly fall in water, its wings waterlogged. It struggles, fluttering. A fish plays with it, sucks it in, lets it out. The fish seems to have paws. Happy fish bouncing and pouncing in sunlit water enjoying butterfly flutter.

An older boy tells the twelve year old, "There's a lot of death in nature. Nature is big on death." The twelve year old becomes a vegetarian, can't bear the idea of murdering animals.

Is Plotinus right, after all? Matter is evil? What of mangled spirit? For Plotinus, mangled spirit is (mis)identification with matter, a lower level of soul. One needs to set oneself aright, discover the higher power, the true self within. True self uplifted by beauty-goodness. Mangled spirits? Leave them rotting on the road.

My twelve year old is not a mangled spirit but sees mangled spirits clearly, feels them within. Their eerie glows wax and wane. He is not immune, not above. Punctured by realization, he plunges into life.

My twelve year old loves the body that pains him, the body that is death, gateway of senses, infinities of feeling. The senses — messengers of goodness. There is joy planted in the body, joy of spirit. My twelve year old is appalled by life, but life embraces him.

Plotinus is not wrong. Beauty-goodness, true core of cores. In every pore. Melding with agony. Licking mangled spirit with originary waves. Agony is baseline fact. Craters of joy mark it. I betray my twelve year old with a sensation of rarefied goodness-beauty. Where does it come from, surrounded by agony? When does agony fuel the brightly burning flame? When does it make the flame go out? For my twelve year old, no distillation of beauty nullifies pain. He does not detach beauty from suffering. If Plotinus is ashamed of his body, Walt Whitman sings the body electric, the joy of pores. Where is Whitman's shame, Plotinus's body ecstasy? How long could agony exist if secret joy were not sewn in the shatter? Even in agony, one expects life. One expects everything between pulses of pain.

The twelve year old I'm learning from makes no concessions. He does not betray his pain. He does not pretend it isn't what it is. Many say it shouldn't be this way, but it is. His life has pleasures, joys. Not Platonic. His life gives the lie to pure beauty. Joy is part of everyday pain. He loves life without turning shit to gold. A moment is gold enough. He lives-gives what he is. Everydayness—more than enough.

A woman tells me she has no vision of light, nothing seeable within. But she's always had a sense of Something More, a spiritual sensation she never gave up on, that never gave up on her.

She tells me her early life was horrible. Everyone in her family put everyone else down, fighting all the time. Predatory, pecking orders, who's on top-bottom, all-consuming. Life has to be more than this.

Work is no different. Everyone trying to be better than everyone else, compete, get ahead, put down, climb on top. Like her family.

Does anyone care about anyone?

She works in institutions. Patients in and out. Suicides. Make the numbers look good. Don't do what really needs doing. Follow guidelines. Guidelines less and less humane.

She can't live this way. There must be Something More.

Years of depression, anxiety.

She can't change the predatory system.

But Something More holds fast. Not a voice, not a light. Something real nonetheless, more real than the predatoriness of things.

So many years she feels useless. She tries, fails. What good is Something More if nothing happens, if things get worse and worse. She sees the basis for Armageddon in the facts of life.

She is a fool for trying, a fool for sensing.

Years go by. Something More persists.

A little here, a little there — Something More does not let go.

Less depression, less anxiety. An opening, a movement.

Something More happens in little ways, very little. An impalpable sensation — nothing more real. "It's there all the time," says my patient, with appreciative wonder. "I felt dumb speaking for it. It's taken forty years to begin." It's taken so many years to appreciate her sense of life, its taste of Something More.

There is Something More built into her sense of life, Something she always knew was there but more or less kept hidden, a secret from herself, a secret she secretly appreciated. She was afraid of it, ashamed of it, but it grew and she grew with it, many, many years. Even though she believes little may be done against the dominant tide (the money-mad, vicious Nothing More), she is amazed to see Something More working in people around her, even in those she felt against her. Something More keeps working, even if the dominant tide drowns it. It works in the drowning. Cruelty is pervasive. But Opening happens. People are helped. Lives are lifted. Not all mangled spirits are left to rot on the roadside.

For my patient, this does not mean assent to the way things are: she will never assent, any more than will my twelve year old. But she can pour whoever she is into whatever she's able to do. Some do this from the beginning. Some take many years to find ways to start.

In my early thirties I visited by Aunt Bert while she was dying. She was bitter. "I didn't think it would happen so soon, Mike, not like this," she moaned. An incisive, slicing moan cutting through life. I held her hand, put my hand on her forehead. Cancer ate her body away. Her bony fingers looked for her genitals. Her body wanted to become a fetus. It wanted to find a way to be comfortable. I stayed a long time, and time faded. I could not tell where life left off and death began. I could not tell the difference between life and death. A glow suffused bitterness. A bitter glory. A weeping love. How could any joy be in the room? It grew and grew, and there was no more life or death.

A few months later, still in awe of these moments, I made an appointment for the first physical checkup of my adult life.

An artist suffers extreme joy in working. Extreme agony. She packs her canvas with colors, blackens them out, layers, starts again. She turns the canvas toward the wall and stares at its back. She cannot finish it. She destroys it repeatedly. She returns to it for months. It has been many paintings, many works — it has passed through many identities and destructions of identities. It is never right.

She feels she does this with her lovers. They do it themselves — go through layers of identities, nothing right.

She speaks easily with friends. She is a good friend, a wonderful friend, but is impacted in herself. "Stuffed. Jammed. Nothing comes out. What comes out is not what needs to."

We go over old ground, but what's the use. A case of impacted feelings. She learned from an early age to hold feelings in, keep them secret. For her father, she needed to act normal, healthy, competent. He laughed at her emotions if she showed them. She is very competent. She loses track of how split she is. Deep inside, impacted life. Outside, terrific competence, amiable well-being, caring ability.

With her mother there was crazy emotionality — demanding, active, invasive, chaotic. She learned that pure emotionality is destructive. Her father was right to want the threatening stream withheld. Her mother was right in storming his rational self-confidence.

Where does this leave *her*? Caught between? Nowhere? A pithy, subdued combination? An original? Layering and blackening canvases. Telling me she cannot find a way to speak to me.

There is ghastly pain unable to speak, ghastly ecstasy bound in the pain. The joy of colors drowning in black. Will the black be dull? Will it glisten?

Isaac, Abraham's son, digger of wells, traumatized by the knife. Must he fill the wells with sand and cement them over before he can draw water? Sarah's son, bitter laughter. My patient's wells are deep. Some surface, refreshing friends, while she drowns in thirst.

She is furious that her latest boyfriend tries to solve his problems with medication. She cannot stand his "good" moods. She cannot feel *him*. He ignores the lasting, problematic nature of her thirst, thinking it easy to appease. Won't good feeling do? She feels he's lifted off his baseline. Agony needs to be met with agony, if joy is to be joy. Her psychic modem seeks complexity, not a clean slate with a buzz.

"Everything collapses into a word or experience, a density. I'd like it to be the opposite. With friends I can say *more* than I usually feel. I can say *more* than I'm consciously thinking about. Here it's totally opposite. I can't say where I am. I sense a lot of feelings, but they're paralyzed. I'm in pain all the time."

She's always been able to function above the pain, live above the pain, as her boyfriend does with medication.

"Emotionally impacted. I'm going to explode. I'm paralyzed."

Explosive paralysis–paralyzed explosion.

"I'm upset. Scatter off to another direction. Scared. Annoyed at myself, at you. It's never been this bad."

Another patient tells me she sees stuff packed into her ears, "packs of lies," a phrase her father used repeatedly. Packs of lies. Yucky stuff in her ears. "You're told this and that, all the phony stuff to make you behave this way, that. You're scared into being this or that. You become a pack of lies."

My painter is stung by truth, paralyzed by impacted truth. Impacted truth. Impacted lies. All the things you swallow, stuff in your ears, in your belly, in your paintings, in your poems, in your therapy. Digging, burying, covering, opening.

Her wings grow back when she leaves my office.

Some people find wings in therapy. Some find clot after clot.

"My wife tells me I'm much better." The man who tells me this is more natural, spontaneous at home, gets more pleasure in work. In therapy he has been nearly silent for seven months. He goes nowhere, impacted, clotted. He says the clot is reddish. Sometimes there is a golden halo emanating from it. Sometimes a pulsating clot, sometimes an inert clot.

We sit and watch the clot on the floor between us.

Strange way to spend time.

The black shines through the colors, the colors through the black. They interlace, fight, commingle, compete, radiate. Her paintings deepen, demand more perceptive-apperceptive leaps, speak to something impacted in people, something that blackens color, that requires incubation time. She is, finally, changing through her work. It is easier to work than look one's work in the eye and be seen by it. Something is happening. Our sessions are impacted clots.

To be swallowed by impacted areas opens subtle areas of uncontrol, deeper unknowability. In my painter's case, new phases of work and life, always with the possibility of aborting, too much to take. Little entries where joy and pain are one, blackness-brightness one.

Leila tells me she's been feeling free, soaring like an eagle. A variable, persistent ecstasy for days, weeks. The best time of her life. She's gone through hells, still goes through hells, not quite the same hells. The ecstasy waxes-wanes, with greater-lesser intensity, but its presence is nearly constant. Then she sees herself in a mirror, an old Jewish woman. It's shocking but doesn't get her down for long.

She doesn't look especially old to me, but I know what she means. The split between inner and outer can be enormous.

Actually, I'm nearly a decade older than she. An old Jewish man. The ecstasy waxes-wanes, nearly constant. So does a depressive streak. Both together. They coincide, pull apart somewhat, overlapping circles, tug at each other, create tension, embrace each other, create textures and tonality. I've grown to love them both, distrust them both.

Sometimes the split has an opposite effect. There are times I'm falling apart, breaking to pieces, falling through space, disappearing. This is bad enough. What makes it worse is the evil, monstrous aspect — times when I fall into a sense of evil, misshappeness, deformity. In inner vision my face seems ugly, twisted, its worst infinitized, distorted in ghastly ways. An image of utter madness, warped, poisoned-poisonous, broken, crippled. Spinning into a hideous oblivion, a malignant dying that threatens to go on forever. The pain becomes unbearable, and consciousness begins to blur, blot out, become unconscious.

There are moments like these when I look in the mirror and my actual face doesn't look nearly as bad as my face in inner vision. "That's not so bad," I say to myself. My face looks good, together, strong — not falling apart or warped. Somehow I feel better, snap back to myself. Seeing my face in the mirror gives me a sense of unexpected relief and cohesion. I come together again, feel just plain me, saved by the image in the mirror. At such a moment, the image in the mirror makes me real.

There appear to be two contrasting inner Platonic selves and complementary outer perceptions of face. A person may feel beautiful or ugly, free or disintegrating — a variation of Plato's black and white horses. Horrific-beatific inner faces and selves. Wondrous beauty and near absolute ghastliness. Either can be confirmed or disconfirmed by external perception.

In Leila's case, inner freedom and beauty are disconfirmed by outer aging, with its penumbra of mortality, fragility, ugliness. She was brought up short by the discrepancy between inner and outer vision, soaring like an eagle, looking like a hag. In my case, an inner spin into absolute and hideous agony was offset by a reminder of outer solidity. It could go either way.

Four obvious logical possibilities, all of them real: inner ugliness disconfirmed by outer goodness and vice versa; inner ugliness or beauty confirmed by outer ugliness or goodness.

I suppose it is especially nice when inner and outer beauty or goodness meet each other, so that good feelings are mated with external perception, and one goes on feeling good. This can be abused if the evil image is foreclosed and one imagines one really is as good as one looks or looks as good as one feels. In the worst scenarios, there is no room for disconfirmation. One creates a solid circle that seals the self and renders one immune to the feelings of others.

I've supervised therapists who, at times, feel too good for their patients. Feeling too good about oneself can blind one to the bad feelings of others. One needs to place limits on ecstasy in order to experience another's difficulties.

Still, for a soul not used to feeling *and* looking good to oneself, a new sense of inner-outer goodness coming together is a blessing indeed. The opposite condition often is permanently devastating—feeling ugly inside *and* seeing oneself as ugly outside. I don't mean only or merely physical ugliness but a kind of psychological viability or worth. What is most devastating about inner or outer ugliness is not simply physicality, although that counts, but the bad psychic taste one has of oneself. As if one's very self tastes bad and one is, essentially, repulsed by oneself.

It is also possible—I fear this is not too uncommon—that a therapist may feel an all too real fit between a person's inner and outer ugliness. For example, a person may be a bully and act and seem bullyish. Hitler as a patient might have conveyed such an impression in the extreme. The problem such a person presents to a well-meaning therapist can appear insuperable. Often a person is unable to perceive or approach his bully self in any serious way. The inner-outer bully is bathed in a sense of righteousness. At most, this individual goes back and forth between extremes of impermeable righteousness—bully par excellence—and drops into sniveling anxiety or depressive bouts blamed on external circumstances (something impedes the full realization of bullyhood).

Much therapeutic work goes into establishing and cultivating variably confirming-disconfirming visions of self. We are made up of multiple systems and capacities that cross-check, balance, enrich, and fight each other. It is an impoverished plight to be stuck with one or two views of self. Black and white horses within provide initial supplementary takes on any moment. Inner-outer visions confirm-disconfirm each other in complexly evolving ways.

It is difficult to establish rules. Sometimes oversimplifying oneself is adaptive. One reduces self in order to survive. But being able to pursue many views of self opens possibilities of living. One needs an array of confirmations and disconfirmations of inner- and outer-oriented states for richness of life.

Any one thought is part of a hidden network of thoughts. Any one feeling is part of a context of feelings. Any vision leads to, departs from, grows in relation to previous and future visions, variably conscious-unconscious. It is freeing, if disconcerting, to realize that there are always other courts of appeal within and outside the self. Learning to enjoy and work with the multiplicity and plurality within does not save one from problems of selection. But it enlarges the tone, resonance, and scope of anguish.

There are body ecstasies and transcendental ecstasies. Fear-rage ecstasies, erotic ecstasies, intellectual ecstasies, power ecstasies, hate ecstasies, love ecstasies. There is free-floating ecstasy almost any capacity can trigger and dip into. Hitler ecstasies. Saint Teresa ecstasies. Incessant amalgams of selfishness-surrender, twin ecstatic poles. Sensation, feeling, thinking, intuition, willing, imagining, believing, disbelieving, knowing, unknowing — all ecstasy vehicles. Do we have a clue what this is all about, what to do with it?

Jenny asks, "Will I ever get a guy?"

In the half dozen years she's seen me we've gone through a lot together. She's run through a number of guys and vice versa. Her relationships follow a common pattern: first, the ecstatic thrill, then moments of ecstasy if the erotic element goes well, and ecstasies of walking, talking, being together in the electricity of the city; then the pain, blossoming into agonies. In and out of ecstasy-agony for weeks or months, until pain prevails. Doubt, loss, self-questioning: what's wrong with me? Failure, shatter.

When therapy started, the failure-shatter phase was sickeningly drawn out, punctuated with minor ecstatic flare-ups in the midst of hope, longing, and regret. Endless self-torture. Within a couple of years, therapy enabled the end phase to end sooner and be less devastatingly consuming and emptily prolonged. In a couple of more years, therapy enabled Jenny to jump not quite as high when the thrill bell rang, particularly when it was obvious the relationship was doomed. Where did that leave her? Alone? Wary? Cautious? Cut off?

The truth is she was even more cut off before, more cut off from self. Previously, she was in tune with bits of self that tyrannized her, inflamed her, broke her. She came to see me in the wake of a hospitalization for a serious breakdown. Erotic flare-ups, of the sort outlined above, partly pasted her together as preconscious fears of falling apart mounted. For years she navigated around personality "faults," avoiding breakdown by transient erotic hits, relationships that almost worked, always falling short, leaving her stranded. It almost seemed as if being agonizingly stranded in a long, drawn-out way kept her together. She complained, longed, felt miserable, had orgies of self-deprecation, as if tantalization and loss were needed as personality glue.

We had gone through enough for me to say, "Whether destiny, fate, or luck will bring a man, one sure partner you have in life is you. You have to be with you. You have to spend time with yourself."

Jenny tells me how many times she almost ended it—just because she was with herself, sentenced to herself. This is old ground, real but old. The new thing she spoke of is not picking on herself as she used to. "I'll probably always pick on myself. I can't help it. But there's a huge difference. I pull out of tailspins. I pull out of it faster. I come through the shatter. Sometimes I recognize myself; sometimes I'm different. I'm less afraid of being less recognizable. I know I'll come back one way or another. I'll be there, one or another version. I almost look forward to the changes shatter can bring, otherwise I'd feel so same, so deadly bored with myself."

"I make myself laugh," she continues, thinking she is not so bad to be with. "I have many thoughts. I like being with myself. Time I spend alone is interesting. But the attacker comes: What did I do wrong? Guys at work speak about their dates. One right in front of me talks about the most terrific date he's had in years. Some terrific, young, sexy girl for sure. I feel awful. I know on the spot the attacks will build as soon as I'm alone. They'll get louder. I'm not pretty enough, smart enough, emotional enough, too emotional, too smart, not sexy enough, too hungry—just plain *not* or *too*.

"Dare I say it? I feel happy a lot of the time. I feel good going to work, doing things by myself or with friends. If I'm alone on the weekends, I find things to do. I like my apartment, listening to music, sketching, following the moment. It really does feel good to be alive. I wasn't always able to say that. I like being me a lot better. Then the attacker makes me feel being alone is a punishment, proof something's wrong with me. I try to think my way out of it—a lot of people are punished a lot worse for far stupider things. I think my mother made me feel anything wrong with me was my fault, like getting scars not taking care of my acne with medicines when I was a kid. Everything bad that happens to me is my fault. I should have taken better care of myself, made myself different. Whatever I do is wrong. Whatever happens is a punishment.

"I feel so many blessings in my life. My life's a blessing. But in the punishment mind life's a curse, so many curses. Now I feel more a blessing than a curse. Curses come inside the blessings. I guess I'm stuck with a better permanent partner than before. Before the spins didn't stop, the punishment went on and on. I think of my blessings. I'm fun to be around. I live in the greatest city in the world and can afford to do things occasionally. There are many things I enjoy. The main curse is the man situation.

"I did some really good work yesterday and last night at home. I jogged in the park this morning, felt great. Even now I'm buoyed up more than when I came in. I'm ready to go to work, look forward to it. I really like it and love the people I work with. Yet when I stop to think — it's been a few years since I had a boyfriend. I think of my married cousins.

"I could be feeling really good, and my mother calls and says maybe I should get another shrink or move to another city. Maybe I should move back with them. Maybe I should give up everything I built because it's the wrong everything. It's not the everything she wants for me.

"I'm sitting in the middle of my happiness and my mother says I'm living the wrong life. Where's the man, the children, the family? My father says maybe I work too hard and I'm not soft enough and men are afraid of me. Maybe I should put ads in the paper, take a charm class, find more male tennis partners. Spend less time working, more time dating."

Jenny depicts a good everyday feeling, a real achievement supported by our being together, year after year, going through hells, letting goodness resurface after being defaced. She feels her bliss under attack. She can spot the attacker a mile away. She sees it coming, knows the drill. She has faith in goodness at the heart center, currents of well-being, satisfaction in being alive. She *knows* there is this center, this satisfaction, and believes in it, even as the attacker riddles it with doubts. Riddles, ridicules, rids life of goodness.

Her breakdown occurred because the attacker won. The love point at the center got beaten down, overrun. Her breakdown was a scream of loss, defeat, a horrible cry: the soul Nazis might win forever. There could be no business as usual unless repair began. Self-feeling needed to be restored, slowly won back from *not* and *too*. After six years, we are still beginning. But no longer beginning from the same place.

Any number of times Jenny got suckered into dating someone her parents told her about. She used to be enamored of glitzy guys they liked. Her only long-term relationship was with a plainer, simpler guy they recoiled from. What was she doing with *him*, they asked. She could do better.

Little did she know she would never do better. She liked him and he liked her. They had good times together. He loved her very much, and she felt love for him too but wasn't sure. Mostly her doubts hinged on the idea of doing better. The actual, lived reality with him was pretty good. She broke up to do better. He went on to have a fine career and family, while she chased glitzy guys who couldn't love. She opted for image over love, confused the two, until her breakdown.

"I'm still doing it," she says. "I can't believe I went out with a guy my parents fixed me up with this weekend. A bomb, of course. As always. I never learn. There was no way anything real could happen between us. I wouldn't even want it too. I still fall into what they want for me. I think I want it too. Not as badly as I used to—not as long. I saw pretty quickly what I was doing.

"Their anxiety is some kind of noise that rattles me. It takes me out of myself, breaks down my good feeling. It's not only them. It's society, peer pressure, the supposed to's. Of course, it *would* be good to marry, have a family—for true fulfillment. Not for peer, parental, social, biological, and gene pressure—but my personal self. But if not, for whatever reasons—lack of fit between the kind of person I am and the world now, whether it's place, temper, looks, something deeper—the most important thing of all is the life-feeling I have, true life-feeling, sense of self and cosmos."

"My parents couldn't bear my decomposing. They couldn't let me be sad or anxious or brood or do nothing. Anger was OK. They took anger as a sign of strength. You assert yourself, seem together. You're someone when you're angry, not when you're anxious, at a loss, drifting.

"I've been in a fog my whole life and acted like I was on top of things. I had to look good, act like I knew what I was doing. I did enough things well to hide the fog, make believe it wasn't there. My parents couldn't take it.

"I became an integration freak, acting more whole than I felt. I felt more together than I was. My ability to be good at things made me feel together. I learned to make friendships work, even with people I wouldn't want to be friends with. I carried it too far and broke down. There wasn't a place in my life I could be a mess. Then the mess took over.

"Does everyone know about this? Is it something I'm learning that everyone knows? You don't pressure me to be together, to be someone. You let me drift or be frightened or sad or not be at all. You tell me it's OK to be unintegrated. You don't seem frightened when I decompose. Does anyone know about this? Decomposition therapy. It's a relief."

"All my life I felt above everyone. I was staying above myself. I think my parents feared little breakdowns would lead to bigger ones. The opposite is true. The big breakdown came because I couldn't let down a little at a time. The big breakdown exaggerated the little ones I didn't have.

"So much pressure to be integrated. Defensive integration. It failed to hold up. Trying to be above costs a lot. I was afraid to be below."

I felt Jenny's pressure ebb a little. For the moment, I felt lower than everyone. A lowly worm. Free. No reason to climb, to exert myself. Just make my way in the mud, the gruel, the grime. Let others be better, more, strained. Let it all fall away.

Jenny smiled. She seemed a little dazed, relaxed, open, quietly appreciative, not quite sure what would be next. Her face had the gentle yielding that a body feels after prolonged illness, when the fever breaks.

33

"Some days I come in here like a worm cut up in bloody pieces going in different directions. By the time I leave my spirit feels buoyed. I don't know why I feel buoyed but I do."

I remember many days Jenny came with false hopes, false highs, thrills that ended up cutting her. Now she leaves with a modicum of peace, not just in pieces. She is beginning to taste new nuances of the mystery of what people can do to one another, new currencies of feeling.

"I dreamt I was dusting the outside of cabinets," says Dalia.

She speaks of poetry she is working on, her blocks, struggles, joys. Suddenly, she thinks of her love of Saint Teresa's writings. "They inspire me. I'm in awe of them. She goes all the way, as far as you can go. She follows the true self to the end." Dalia speaks of Saint Teresa's mystical journey and concludes rather self-deprecatingly, if truthfully, "I'm not able or willing to work that hard."

"Poetry is dusting off the true self," I say.

"Therapy, too?" she asks. "I guess I'm just dusting the outside. Saint Teresa gets inside the cabinets, she opens them, she goes deep into them. She dusts off the true self to completion. But it's also something to dust the cabinets."

To be a cabinet duster is no shame.

Creative imagination can be evil. I think of one person seeing a patch of color or beauty in another and taking off on it.

One day Beth saw Karen and began to go on about a lovely red in her blouse. Beth got carried away, likening it to this or that angel, this or that psychological trait and spiritual meaning, a particular, precious red of deep mystical import.

Karen was old and ill and in pain. She could hardly walk. Her body was a source of misery. Beth went on and on. Karen felt totally unseen. She passed by unnoticed, while Beth's wings beat wildly.

I once saw a print of Tamayo's painting called *Happy Mother*. The mother had a hideously ecstatic, if monstrous, expression as she embraced her baby. The baby was pinned to her breast with arms outstretched like those of Jesus crucified.

Ecstasy is more than enlightenment.
Enlightenment is more than ecstasy.

Inside a pinched and contracted person everything is boundless.

There is a Light of lights, and when one sees it no questions remain.
There is nothing more beautiful.
One feels secure, trust.
One is satisfied in the Light's presence, whatever death is.
Whether one lives on in some form or other, goes through hell, purgatory, heaven or nothing, or never lives again — one lives forever now.
One asks nothing of the Light, no more than just to be.
Who shall I say sends me, asks Moses. Tell them Just Is sends you.
I do not know if the Light heals illness, makes for longevity or success, or does anything except bring a smile in your heart.
Truth is, I may not be aware of smiling or not. Just a kind of seeing and feeling.
Is it inside or out? In skin, pores, self, imagination? A visual component — the Light itself. Chest feeling suffusing skin, limbs, spreading.
Maybe I can feel the Light more intensely when I'm alone. Not necessarily. It helps me see others more clearly. I can feel the truth of another's life, the Light shining in, over, through the other, the poignancy of a whole life, beauty-tragedy, love, anguish, joy taking form, passing. The Light simply is. A blessing. It blesses, calms fears, adds holiness. Talking about it is good, but when I see it there are no descriptions or demands.

I have spent many therapy sessions looking at the Light in-around-over-through a person or between us. I've also spent many sessions fatigued, heavy, groggy, ornery, not quite there, waiting for time to be up. I at least try not to take my states out on others, but I am not always very successful. We pick up the pieces as best we can.

Once an ornery patient who doesn't believe in therapy confronted me: "What are you doing in my sessions? Looking at the Light?"

"Yes," I said. "When I'm lucky."

This person was a mess when he started therapy. He and I are messes now, but we can be lighter about it. His life has gotten better. He is not in as much pain. He has a mate, children. Work goes better. He feels more human. When I met him, he was in agony most of the time, an agony that went nowhere. He chewed himself up. His relationships backfired. Work was ominous.

He got mad at me a lot for not doing real work with him. When he got better, he insisted he would have gotten better anyway. But he knew he was lying. He knew our relationship made a difference.

I saw the Light in his face, the glow, the spark. I gave him room. I liked his eccentricity and waited.

To this day, he makes fun of me and therapy. If we have to miss a session, he is happy to save the money. He likes to think he doesn't need me but fears he does and still gets better.

He now realizes I look at the Light he brings into the room. He jokes about the Light but does not really put it down.

Why couldn't my patient get better by going to a shaman, or a spiritual healer, or dipping into a traditional spiritual path? Why was seeing me necessary? Does psychoanalytic therapy add anything to the Light? The Light certainly adds something to psychoanalytic therapy.

This patient mocks traditional religions. They are empty for him. He is more open to esoteric spiritual phenomena, but they did not help his plight as a suffering being. Therapy seemed more natural for him, even if he mocked it. Perhaps he needed something familiar to mock. Maybe he felt comfortable mocking me because he sensed I could take it and turn it to good use.

He needed to talk about his life, the contradictions of childhood, worries, the torment of being alive, the pain of being the kind of person he was, abysmal failures, partial successes, the catalogue of living. Therapy is a bit like meditating out loud, praying out loud.

Therapy is the butt of a lot of jokes, justifiably. But to go on talking one's life out is more than a luxury. Pictures of self swim into being. Longings grip one. Cries of pain escape one's lips. Joys and triumphs are shared. One does more than get to know oneself better. One gets a "feel" for what one has gone through, might go through. One gets a "feel" for the moment one is, the moment one might be.

Psychoanalytic listening is not duplicated by other paths. Lacan writes that no praxis is more real or tries more to touch the heart of experience. This is not to say psychoanalysis takes the place of making love, sharing reactions to a movie, working, going to a ball game, having a mystical experience. But where else can two or more people focus on how they feel together and explore subtle nuances of these feelings further and further, following them anywhere, beyond the reachable?

That this is done in a secular spirit makes it free. That this is done with a sense of the holy makes it sacred. Everything between people is potentially valuable, almost everything can be put to use. A certain kind of listening and feeling makes this possible. Two people devoted to feeling everything together, discovering limits of honesty: any and all thoughts have valid passports, yet tact reigns.

Lacan teaches that what we know of dreams is only dream traces. The dream disappears behind itself. The images, bits of narrative, affects in dreams give a lot to work with, but more is unrevealed. The unconscious vanishes behind what it offers.

This is simpatico with lines of ancient wisdom: the self disappears at its point of origin. Elusiveness par excellence. Mystery as such.

Freud wrote of a dream navel, a density. The dream arises from, vanishes within its navel. A knot, a cut. What does one find if one passes through the navel of a dream? Is such a passage possible? Is it the only necessary passage?

Lacan uses terms like "cut" and "pulsative" to describe unconscious work. The link with feminine genitals is no accident. Lacan speaks of unconscious processes as "pulsations of the slit." A rhythm of opening-closing working together. The unconscious closes as it opens, opens as it closes.

Freud linked death drive pathology with something wrong with psychic rhythms, timing, flow. Some lack of feminine ecstasy.

Many dreams show dread of penetration. Paranoia is a kind of psychic vaginismus. Pulsation of the slit—feminine ecstasy—is frozen, rigid.

One works to locate dread as a forerunner of surrender. One tries to find what fluid elements of personality remain.

The standard translation of Freud's "Wo es war, soll Ich werden" is "Where id was, ego will be." Lacan speaks against a warrior psyche, where ego dislodges id. His version is more like, "I will go where it is. I will go where you are. I will follow you. I will go with you-it. I'll return to the place of dreams, to the place dreams come from, through the dream navel."

Another formulation might be, "My home is in the field of the unconscious, the unrealized-unrealizable. My home is Mystery."

You are at home in the mystery of the dream,
in the dream navel and beyond.
You are at home where the dream vanishes.

Schreber is right to see in feminine ecstasy a spiritual path. He is fascinated by his desire to be a woman in sexual orgasm, God's sweetheart, divine bride. Surrender competes with terror, rape, murder, loss. Something has gone terribly wrong. There is too much evil for the pulsative rhythm to work. Shifting battlelines are drawn between surrender and control. Trauma intensifies and mutilates longing and loss.

Boris: "There's a hole I fill with drugs, work, marriage, affairs, therapy. Nothing fills it. I'm a control freak. I need to be boss. I can't listen to anyone. I'd like my whole life to be a therapy session, everyone centered on me. I go on talking."

Boris is terrific working with addicts. He helps people. He's also a great administrator. He's good at math and contributes immensely to organizing programs for addicts. People appreciate his sense of mastery, his ability to take charge, put things together.

He enjoys taking control, but people also appreciate him because he leaves room for them to live their lives. They appreciate the structure he provides, his clearheaded sense of what would work better. He is a good coach. He tries to get people to do good things for themselves and favor healthy over destructive tendencies.

Boris is not heavy-handed. He has a light touch. He enjoys playing with ideas, dreams, fantasies, perspectives. He is good at dancing with people mentally, sometimes to their consternation, often to their delight. He is able to give room — while being controlling — because he is extremely detached. Something is missing. He doesn't feel real.

"I'm great at parties because I'm so detached. It's a game; it doesn't matter. I like to have a good time. I enjoy myself because nothing counts."

Boris talks about things he does well, like partying, making money, controlling self-destructive people. Yet there is the emptiness. I think of Fred Astaire's detachment. He could stand above himself and observe his body working. I think of dispassionate detachment in aspects of cultural theory and practice. Boris has a germ of it, but he is at a loss. He is missing the "feel" of his life. And he is good at watching himself miss the feel of his life.

He is no ordinary empty person. He believes in bliss. Joseph Campbell's "Follow your bliss." He is good at it, although, too often, the hole swallows the bliss or comes back after the bliss. Still, he has not given up. He is dedicated. He believes bliss is real, the hole unreal. Unreality often is stronger and cancels the real. Boris's belief prevents him from slipping into unreality permanently and keeps him on a decent track. He has learned, the hard way, that trying to do good makes his life easier and more comfortable than indulging compulsive destructiveness. It is more practical to stay on the good side, if possible. He lives a kind of psychic mathematics, a practical kind of transcendence characterized by calculation and control. I sense a basic goodness in him, which he acknowledges. It operates without filling him.

He is devoted to his children, but they do not fill the hole. He feels most real with them, up to a point. Detachment remains and sooner or later takes over. His children feel frustrated by his detachment and emotional vanishing, but benefit from his discernment and goodwill. His emptiness is double-edged. It helps and frustrates people, especially his children and himself.

A sticking point between us is that he does not believe in agony. "Where's the missing agony?" I ask. He smiles a trifle condescendingly. "I lost it long ago," he tells me. "I learned to live without it." He depicts a mother who teased him with chaos. She was turmoil itself. Not benevolent turmoil, but injurious, abusive, controlling. He feels she was unavailable as a person but needed to stick him with her personality quills, as she tried to pour herself into him. His father practiced disappearing. At his best moments he displayed a blank encouragement tinged with indifference. I looked for pools of hidden love in Boris's tale, but he assured me he turned off in the face of love's insufficiency. Turning off feelings became a habit, and the habit became reality.

It took many destructive years before Boris pulled out of the spin. There were years he feared he'd kill himself with drugs or self-annihilating behavior. A self-survival thread prevailed and, after false starts, got his life on track. He saved his life and found ways of living with those he cared about, but lost the feel of himself. You'd think, if he had the sense and ability to right himself, a feel for himself must be working. I believe this is so, yet not a reality for him. He lived without a feel for himself and learned to make things decent enough, in case he ever showed up. Boris was unflinchingly honest about his condition, and this tended to win me over.

Is it possible to recapture the "feel" of self without discovering agony? Pain is one thing, agony another. Boris feels there's no profit in agony. He sees people addicted to useless suffering. Suffering is something to fill the hole. He cannot let the hole be agonizing. It simply is a somewhat painful fact. There is no sense to agony: sound and fury signifying nothing. He can entertain the notion that his agony was too much to bear, that it was senseless, endless, unprofitable. But this is theory. In fact it is gone, or never was, nothing, possibly a dull pain waxing-waning in the background. Boris cannot cry. Is it, also, that he *will* not cry, that something refuses to crack? Or that he has reached a point beyond cracking, where the idea of cracking no longer applies?

Wayne consults me about his therapy. He loves his therapist but being with her is too painful. He feels she is friendly, competent, distant. She wants him to emote but withholds herself.

He is recovering from a previous therapy, in which his therapist solicited deep dependency, then dropped him. She opened him up but didn't want to deal with his unending sensitivity and vulnerability. His ensuing depression, paralysis, and neediness frightened her, became oppressive, and she ended treatment.

Was he too much for a therapist?

Apparently he is not too much for another human being. He is in a fifteen-year relationship with his partner, Jim. They've learned through trial and error how to live together and continue learning. Wayne is mad that his current therapist is not open to learning. Why can't she find ways of negotiating an emotional relationship with him? She pulls back, retreats into professionalism.

He can't stand the one-way quality of therapy. "It's as if someone's looking at me from another room through a one-way mirror." This might be tolerable if his therapist would not insist that relationship is two-way, that they create an emotional field together, that what goes on between them is crucial. It infuriates him that she says one thing, does another. Two-way for him, one-way for her.

He confesses, she analyzes. "She shows how my feelings toward her relate to my family in the past and how my feelings toward others relate to her now. It drives me crazy, although I get something from it, a sense of order. I don't think it's the analyzing I mind, but her use of it to deflect away from her feelings. Just when I think I'm going to have feeling-to-feeling contact, she tells me what my feelings mean. That's useful, I know. But it stops something; it short-circuits a flow. Sometimes feelings are more important than what they might mean."

Wayne paused to see how he affected me and to see if he agreed with himself or could catch a false note. "She tells me we are just two people in the room together and what we feel with each other counts. But she invites me to spend most of the time in aerial vision, above, seeing what I feel, making sense of it. I understand there's to be a back-and-forth, experiencing and analyzing. But it's all eyes trained on me from high above. I want something more than someone watching. I want to be felt too.

"I can see she feels me and she says she does. But she jumps away too quickly, starts thinking too soon about what she was beginning to feel, makes interpretations, shares ideas. They're pretty good, that's not the point. She's good at it. But just feeling, being a feeling being—I need more of that. All this focusing on my feelings makes me feel left out."

"Have you talked with her about this?" I ask.

"Yes, often. At times she seems open to feeling but ends up pulling rank. She stops whenever she wants, if it's too much for her, and turns it on me. She's not honest about it. It's in the guise of helping me, not that it's too much for her. She gets out of it. A couple of times she was honest enough to say she needs to be active. She feels alive when she's active. She can't sit still and let it build. She has to do something or feel false. She does not want to get enmeshed with me. She does not want to become formless with me.

"I like her saying this. I get some clue as to what is happening for her. It's better to know her limits, so I don't feel bad for wanting something else. If she doesn't want what I want, fine. I can take that. That's freeing, OK. But analyzing me when she's uncomfortable makes me feel I'm bad for wanting what I do."

Wayne does not know if he can continue therapy. If he leaves, the end will not be as traumatic as last time. Whatever is wrong, his therapist persists. She may close off but does not kick him out. She works, in keeping with herself, as best she can. He will have to be the one who leaves. He may feel that she drove him out by not being open enough. But he knows she is willing to keep trying. This makes a difference.

I feel Wayne's anguish. Questions form, but I resist them. He tells me about the first time he saw his therapist. She gave a talk at a meeting about therapy being an alive encounter based on feeling interchange between two people. The therapist is not a blank screen. As Wayne went on, I thought how mixed our field is. So many therapists caught between old and new paradigms melded together. Everything in transition. A therapist goes back and forth between old and new, sorting things out as she goes along. How caught one can be without knowing it. I suspect things are even more difficult than Wayne imagines. I feel so blocked by my personality. One can be hemmed in by a thought or feeling or will or belief or style of imagining.

"You're telling me how painful your therapy is," I venture. "You seem to understand that its binds reflect binds you've been trapped in. Its binds are more benign but still devastating. The stakes mount as you open up. You feel cheated by her stinginess and fear, nourished by her bravery and good intent. You feel invited to a feast she hides from. Her professionalism helps you but is a tease. Maybe all therapy falls short, but you feel impelled to find out for yourself. You're not satisfied with generalizations. What can a therapy relationship bear? What can it do? How far can it go? We are trying to find out."

"Is life a promise it can't fulfill?" Wayne wonders. "I don't think that's it. It's not what's bothering me. I think I know that on some level. I took anti-depressants after my last therapy. They got me over a hump but stole something away. They drew a line through me I couldn't get underneath. They raised me above something I needed. I've stopped taking them. I'd rather feel grief. I'd rather feel awful, if I can take it. I need my sub-basement to feel real. Staying above the line feels better but not as real. My therapist is nervous about my having gone off meds. She feels my unhappiness with her is related to not taking medication. She wants me to go back on. I say she wants me on medication to knock out the feelings therapy is stimulating. We're coming at it from opposite ends. There are real issues, real feelings that need to be met. And she wants meds to handle them."

Wayne is not happy about feeling awful but is willing to follow the misery out. He has faith something will happen. He wants someone to have faith with him. His therapist frankly tells him she does not believe in so much agony. It is not her way. Wayne has a different intimation. He has a sense of coming through the worst. He has already come through something ghastly and feels there is more to go. As he speaks, he starts to weep. I realize that for some time his speaking has been an angry weeping. He shows himself through his weeping. He is crumbling in the Light. I feel his dedication. He will not stop before he is ready. Perhaps he will never stop.

What if one spends his whole life getting ready? What if one weeps all life long? What if Wayne's therapist is right. Seal it and get on with it.
Wayne is willing to bet everything on a moment of Light.
What if grief keeps him in touch with Light all life long?
What if grief is Light stretching from head to toe?
There are times when grief subsides and Light is everything.

Big mind–small mind.
Big heart–small heart.
In the mixmaster.

Lauren says, "I think more clearly here than anywhere else. You create an atmosphere where thinking happens. Thoughts can come together. If I could do this elsewhere, I'd be able to write."
Lauren also tells me she is incorporating pieces of her body into her body ego. "It's never been done. Pieces of my body coming together. Thumb, stomach, spine — I think I eat so many odd things that are bad for me — I can't resist — I'm trying to piece my body together. All the odd bits of food I can't say no to are bits of me I can't say yes to."
Piecing mind together.
Piecing body together.
Piecing self together.
Coming together ↔ falling apart. Rhythm, pulsation, double fact. A way of talking about how it feels to be alive or how aliveness moves along. For Lauren, rhythm is ruptured. Therapy is an atmosphere in which psyche can begin to breathe, spontaneous rhythms get a chance to restart: in ↔ out, together ↔ apart.
Lauren feels if what happens in therapy could happen outside therapy, she could write. She wishes she could write. At such moments she forgets that what happens inside therapy happens enough outside

therapy so she can live. Over the years we've been together she's gotten a life, a better life. She is *living*. She is more in life than she imagined possible.

Bliss catches up with torment, although torment never ends.

Torment is a tunnel bliss passes through.

Years ago torment was usual, bliss rare. They were far apart from each other. Bliss had a huge impact because of rarity. Lauren clung to memory of blissful moments with a sense of reprieve. She not only loved bliss for its own sake, but also felt amazing relief at torment in abeyance. It may be natural to wish for bliss to go on forever. But Lauren did not expect more than fragmentary moments when bliss blotted out torment.

It seems miraculous when, over time, bliss infuses, then absorbs torment in everyday ways. Bliss and torment become part of each other, not only split apart. Bliss ↔ torment. Separate ↔ interweaving. Rhythmic back-and-forth. States of fusion ↔ antagonism. Blocked ↔ flowing.

Once a basic rhythm is established, there can be more time when bliss and torment are taken for granted, fade into the background, and life just feels better. How does this happen?

James Grotstein writes of a background subject-object of primary identification, a background support for psychic processes. Therapy provides an atmosphere in which psychic lungs can breathe a kind of psychic oxygen. Many metaphors or images are useable. Circulation: psychic air and blood. Nutrition: psychic nourishment, poison and starvation. Respiratory, cardiovascular, digestive system imagery: flow, process, metabolizing capacity, movement, interdependent autonomy.

No one can eat or breathe for me, but without air or food I cannot eat or breathe.

It is not strange, then, to say we eat and breathe God and each other.

Without a body I can't die or be. Without thoughts, feelings, imaginings — what would I be? Where does the I come from? Is ownership (own-ship) innate?

People who come to see me are filled with blank or tormented I's, or empty holes, an incapacity to feel or flooded by too much feeling. Some fear their destructiveness or bad luck — a compulsion to do things that work against them. Some want more — what they have is not enough or the wrong thing, or they do not live well or could live better.

Often I sit in wonder. How did we get here? What are we doing together? What is happening between us? No wonder a person may tell me I'm not doing enough. Will we give each other a chance for something more to happen?

Something more is always happening but takes time.

A person in pain may contract in an effort to put the pain outside the center of consciousness or outside consciousness entirely. Pain and consciousness may be confused with each other, so that consciousness goes on contracting in an attempt to get rid of itself.

We have the kind of consciousness that tries to get rid of itself and hungers for more and more consciousness.

One of the greatest frustrations is the discovery that consciousness can't get rid of itself. The intoxication of sex, drugs, aggression, or power does not completely do the trick. Mystical experience comes close, but longing-frustration-irritability-rage-dread continue. Consciousness may contract-expand toward an infinitesimal point or infinite boundlessness. It may do both together. But it still is consciousness contracting and consciousness expanding and does not stop being a form of itself.

A psychotic individual may make the awesome discovery that he is still there throughout his psychosis. Part of therapeutic cunning or wisdom is to ally with the one who is still there, the one who may outlast or outflank the psychotic turn, the one who grows to encompass it.

Freud called attention to the witness or observer at the center of a psychotic maelstrom. A "normal" part of consciousness is aware of something awful happening to it. At first a psychotic individual may think he or she can control what is happening, but eventually realizes it is beyond control. Madness can't get rid of sanity, and sanity can't get rid of madness. One sort of consciousness can't totally obliterate another. One is aware of the interplay of "sanity-madness" and develops notions about this interlacing.

One thinks of the ancient puzzle: if one always "halves" the distance and can theoretically "halve" distances infinitely, how does one get from here to there? But one does get from here to there. And each step is just a step.

Consciousness can chop itself infinitely and still is consciousness infinitely chopping itself. Consciousness can go mad and still be consciousness going mad. Consciousness can try to kill itself and still be consciousness trying to kill itself.

Is this a sort of perverse psychological proof of immortality?

Dorian Cairn used to talk about time consciousness being a kind of phenomenological "proof" of the immortality of consciousness. If every conscious moment includes consciousness of present-past-future, and this is so at the moment of death, our "last" moment of consciousness is consciousness of present-past-future continuing on.

This is close to a psychotic individual's vision of consciousness disintegrating. Every fragment is variably dead or alive, like bits of a worm. Split it and split it again and again and get proliferating bits of aliveness or semi-aliveness. I remember Cairn's smile when he imagined consciousness present containing past-future, so every pulse of consciousness future contains another present containing another past-future, infinitely. Consciousness never-ending. More integrating than disintegrating.

Does a murderer try to stop this flow? Does he imagine by obliterating a person he can obliterate consciousness of a person? Literature is replete with examples of ghosts. One is haunted by consciousness of the murdered one. Even if one nearly succeeds in obliterating consciousness of the slain (impossible totality), one fails to obliterate the aliveness of the dead in someone's memory somewhere. It is infuriating to realize a dead person can be more alive than ever. The very act of murdering another's consciousness permanently disfigures one's own. Deformations at the core of character are lasting memorials to any voice of consciousness one tries to still.

A man jumped off a building to end the pain of consciousness. Did he lose consciousness on the way down? On the way down, he did not think so. But when he woke up in the hospital, he realized there was a caesura, a pause. He was conscious of being conscious until there was a gap, a black blank. Upon waking he realized, "My God, I'm still here. I failed." Pain returned, together with disappointment and shocking relief. He had blacked out for a while, a result that might have been achieved by a sleeping pill overnight. He was still there. Consciousness going on like running water. Reconnecting on both ends of the blackout. Time can stop. At least for a time.

But what if I tried to kill myself and, like a big bang, exploded into universes of consciousness? What if an explosion that is meant to end consciousness leads to proliferation, pluralities of consciousnesses? When does explosiveness lead to life? When does it end life? Would trying to kill myself lead to more of myself? The idea of haunting oneself forever is scary indeed. One hopes one could do something better with time and timelessness.

A man tries to smash Michelangelo's *Pietà*, soft and tender depiction of dead Jesus held in Mary's lap. I picture rage against ecstatic surrender, fury at the threat of tender opening. Why should there be comfort in so cruel a life? Murder and succor? New life from death? Let us kill this hope and be done with it, refuse to be tortured any longer. Let us blot out the promise as much as possible.

But the *Pietà* continues to shine.

Aliveness, like self-importance, can be a defense.

There are individuals who play up their sense of aliveness at the expense of other people or other areas of experience. They may use an aspect of aliveness to ward off other aspects, or some grouping of alive feelings to ward off duller ones.

This is obvious with bullies. They feel their sense of aliveness takes precedence. They bully others with their aliveness. They bully themselves. Self-bullying may become apparent if a breakdown of aliveness occurs and desperation escalates. Failure to whip oneself into shape turns into skyrocketing panic. If panic is not recognized as part of aliveness, one feels unrecognizable to oneself.

It seems too obvious to say, but variable mixtures of pain-joy-hate-love-panic-and-fill-in-the-blank are part of the sense of aliveness. Aliveness often is destructive. Religions tell us suffering and bliss are parts of aliveness. Psychotherapy teaches that one part of aliveness is identified with at another's expense. One builds identity on a sector of being and then defends it, a kind of psychic territoriality.

If we are open, we find ways to enrich ourselves through interchanges between regions. But often we must contract and defend points of contraction for survival.

We do not know what to do with our sense of aliveness. Sometimes it leads to horrible things, sometimes great things. To say we are learning may be an overstatement. We don't know what we are doing. But sometimes we try.

Therapy provides an arena to experiment with aliveness-deadness. Still, therapy is real. If something goes wrong, a life can be destroyed. We hope therapy is a self-correctable process. It can be wrenching but marvelous when therapist and patient benefit from deep back-and-forth, when shifting crosscurrents of feelings and attitudes go on reworking each other.

At any moment a therapist may be too alive or dead for a given patient—at a given time, in a given way. And vice versa. Therapist-patient are separate persons but also part of a larger emotional field made up of many regions and kinds of aliveness-deadness sensing each other, feeling each other out. One learns to tone X down, tone Y up, so that more nuances of communication become possible. It feels good to relax one's grip on bits of personality one holds on to and repeatedly fine-tune oneself.

"What's mine is yours," an abuse victim tells her abuser. The words echo through her being. They've been doing so since childhood. She is grown up. She can't say no to anyone. People flood her apartment, abuse her things.

Recently, she discovered a sail in her boat had been cut up. Her friend who did it apologized. She excused him—"What's mine is yours," she heard herself say.

Years of abuse, vagina cut and invaded, by glass, penises, sticks, objects a sick man's fancy found. Her friend loved and frightened and hated her into silence. Dread everywhere.

Tormented identification with a sick man's rapture.

To be grown up is to be freer. No more glass and random objects in the vagina. But no more penises either. To be grown up is to be floundering alone. Friends everywhere, cutting sofas, sails, carelessly taking, taking. Getting filled by garbage friendships. Unconsciously identified with their sick rapture.

Subjugation, power, modulated destruction: part of aliveness. Sick aliveness. Real aliveness.

She will kick them out. She will make aliveness better — she will find ways to make aliveness work. No sickly, sneaky, careless tearing of sails.

"What's mine is yours" — a perverse deformation of "You are that!"

The abuse victim loses faith without losing faith. She is disillusioned without being able to process disillusionment. Her hate of the abuser is not allowed to be effective. Her hate neither wounds nor corrects. She is disillusioned: "You're not what I thought you were." But she is not allowed to be disappointed. Her abuser wants her to continue idealizing him, even after idealization shatters.

The abuser can't stand criticism, can't take being seen as he is. He wants his victim to think he is something better, something grand. She should be enraptured with his abusive activity. She must excuse him.

There is a hidden core of rapture in abuse. A rapturous sickliness.

The fusion of rapture-abuse becomes a kind of personality glue, binding bits of self together, bits of self that acts of sickly rapture shatter. One is always being bound by what shatters one. One becomes addicted to both the binding and the shattering. Sickly rapture becomes torment in the abused.

Milton believed his mother sexually abused him. He could not be sure. He did not have a clear and distinct memory of her actually doing this or that. His body felt it. He felt it crawl through him. He felt it like a dream that clung to the inside of his skin. He felt it in his terror and rage. He felt her coming closer when she was drunk, submerging herself in him, blending with him. A beautiful, stuporous woman, reaching for her child when drink failed.

His father's abuse was more purely psychological. He wanted to be applauded when he finally took Milton to live with him. He wanted to be worshipped for giving Milton a home. He wanted to be loved for how great he was and for the great sacrifice he made. He didn't have a clue how Milton felt or what Milton was dealing with. He put Milton down for being too sensitive, and applauded when Milton toughed it out like he did. He couldn't see the crippled places a bombed-out mother left in her wake, nor the fear or weakness a "strong" father deleted.

Milton was furious with his mother *and* father. But there was no place for the fury to go. His father felt it unjustified and shrugged it off. "You're being a baby," was his estimation. And his mother scarcely knew what was happening. Milton was disillusioned with both parents; but his mother didn't care, and his father could not tolerate criticism.

There was no place in life for real feelings.

What an odd thing to think — no place in life for real feelings. Wasn't his father life itself, bigger than life? Wasn't his father — everything? His father made a big show of living. Aliveness was his name. Women, emotions, struggles, fights, truths — utter fearlessness in the great arena. His father was a massive figure. Why couldn't he love like his father, fight like him, gorge on life like him, speak truth like him? He contracted as his father expanded.

Milton was a grown man by the time he saw me, many years of therapy under his belt. He had his own family and suffered greatly from what he felt were his shortcomings as a father, a husband, a man. It was as if he replaced his father's capacity for enjoying life with his own gift for suffering, a suffering that too often didn't go anywhere, feeding on itself, filling space left by his contraction.

Milton sometimes concluded, "I have no receptor for pleasure. I can't process or digest recognition, praise, enjoyment. Rage drives me to lash out with all the force I can muster, with no effect, so it causes me to disintegrate."

He describes dread and fury at pleasuring a woman. He can give a woman pleasure if he is in total control, if he brings her to orgasm doing what he wants. Otherwise, he tantalizes her, brings her to the point of orgasm and lets her drop. He will do this repeatedly, if she can take it. She must give up all control. He begrudgingly may try to do what she wants, but is furious if he succeeds, as if he is his own rival. He wants to hurt her, and feels some relief if she feels pain.

"When I pleasure a woman the way she asks, I feel impotent rage. If I can let myself feel impotence, I might be better. The ferocity, intensity of the rage and the feelings of its impotence make me sink into oblivion. There's no way to express my impotence with enough force to make a difference. I sink back and become disorganized. This kind of frustration and impotent rage leads to madness. Part of me wants to shake like an animal, shake and shake and shake with it. Another part wants to go to sleep, become catatonic.

"Pain and rage combine to drive me out of my mind. Not just emotional pain — body pains. It hurts so much my organs hurt. I'm an imprisoned person. Any touch triggers rage-pain underneath my civilized exterior. I look smooth, and people compliment me for good things I do. I'm a good father, worker, husband — I give it everything, more than I have. My spine, muscles in my back are inflamed. No respite, no relief. I wish someone would hit my back with a baseball bat with such force that all the vertebrae line up and bring relief, the energy flowing from bottom to top. For a moment I'll feel integrated and pain will stop. Pain never stops. Very frightening, getting older, how broken my body feels. I never talked to anybody about how much pain I'm in. 'Get moving,' I tell myself. If I don't, I'll drop into a dead zone with a weird consciousness. I fought the pain for years. The whole inside of my body is on fire, pain constant."

Such ghastly fusion of stupor-intensity. His father's hyperaliveness (aliveness as defense) unites with his mother's oblivion to produce a fusion of rapture with rage–pain–impotence–weird consciousness–fire. Moments of reprieve in fantasy. A lot of work on self, driving deeper, further, feeling the pain through his body that he inflicts on a woman in abbreviated fashion. Orgasm–pain–oblivion–weird consciousness–rage. His father's aliveness, mother's deadness become an impotent rage intoxication driving him mad. An accomplished, good man ever on the edge of a private madness. A weird, mad ecstasy pinning him to rageful, painful oblivion. Crucifixion doesn't come close.

Milton begins the next session talking about wanting to be the center, like his father. His father reveled in being the center of attention. In groups, with women, at work, with Milton. He was Milton's center rather than the reverse. Milton felt pained fury at not ever being the true center of his father's attention. His father always referred everything to himself—even his love ("Look how great I am for loving my son"). Now when Milton does get recognition, he feels he has no right to it, it's illegitimate. Only his father should be the center. He is tormented by the satisfaction he gets and the love he gives. No matter what he does or how deeply he goes, something in him feels crushed. *He* feels crushed and illegitimate. He has very real ecstasies, but they inevitably pass through, cling to a crushed and disenfranchised sense of self.

Now he speaks of wanting to let his wife be the center—or *a* center. She has that right and he wants to give it to her. She is a good woman, devoted to life, to him, their life together. She deserves better. "If I could, I'd worship her as women were in the old days, the days of the goddess. I'd be in awe of her generative life, her body, her capacity to support life, to nourish. She has a right to my worshipping her, to pleasuring her, to giving her what she wants. She doesn't begrudge surrendering to me. It doesn't frighten her. Surrendering brings her satisfaction—ecstasy. Surrendering brings her excitement and peace. It doesn't make her gag. It doesn't make her want to lash out and bash her beloved. When I feel myself start to surrender I get overwhelmed with disgust, rage, terror. I want to kill, to bash, to murder the feeling. I want to stamp it out. I want to stamp her out. I want to stamp anyone or anything that tempts me to feel that way, that begins to make me open.

"I say I want to be the center. My need to be the center is pulverized. But it's just as true, even more, I'd give anything not to have to be the center. I want to make room for my wife, to give others space, a sense of me not taking up all the room, such longing to give room for the other. I feel her need for me to surrender—and it feels right." Milton was stuck not being able to be or not be the center. He longed with all his being to break through this wall, this sticking point.

"How can I not be in awe of my wife, her body, who she is, her mystery, her beauty? I defend against awe with contempt. It's dreadfully ludicrous. It's like having contempt for trees. How can you not be in awe of trees?"

Milton speaks of awe and reverence, primal feelings. Contempt permeates them, spoils them. He abruptly returns to an old theme: "My father couldn't take any criticism." He connects his father's inability to be criticized with sickly contempt soiling awe and reverence. His father worshipped only himself. He displayed contempt for others. Thus awe was doubly contaminated: (1) to be force-fed someone's self-worship poisons the sense of awe; (2) to be forced to breathe in an atmosphere of contempt spoils the sense of reverence.

At the same time, his father's self-idolatry blocked his ability to hear just how important Milton felt he was. He was so filled with self-importance that he couldn't feel his actual importance to his child. He could not feel his child's feelings. Everything was filtered through his self-worship — even his son's real worshipfulness. Milton's love, appreciation, awe, and reverence stuck in his throat, stung his belly, warped his chest. His father was too filled with himself to recognize the true value of his son's deep love, too filled with self-love to be touched acutely, fully by another's love for him.

"I wanted to be with him, to let him know how important coming to pick me up is [when Milton lived with his mother]. I wanted to say how important he is a thousand times when he picked me up. I wanted to tell him, 'I was holding out for you to come, to take me.' I did hold out. Then he couldn't open his arms or face me — like you walking in and not looking at me. I think I scared him — my feelings scared him and he contracted against it. He was so afraid of it. I want to tell you how important you are to me and am terrified you won't believe me, you'll make light of it, you won't feel me. I'm terrified if you do or don't. Now my wife is not afraid of it, and I won't give it to her. I split it in half — give her some sort of half and give my father the undying love and devotion half. This means I can't give deep love at all, and not anything wholeheartedly.

"He couldn't take my hate or criticism. But he couldn't take my love either."

Jack has been in semicollapse all his life, but it has taken years to manifest. He was a research biologist, had affairs, a marriage, children. Life carried him along. The family disease began to catch up with him in his sixties. He became severely depressed, panicky, desperately needed help.

He is on the soft, gentle side, but he spews streams of invectives, murderous-sexual fantasies of all sorts, words filled with bile. He lives on the edge of suicide. After his father died, he became the "sane" one in the family, taking care of matters, keeping the ship on course. He can't believe he is breaking down — finally.

We have enormous capacity to be supersensitive *and* blunt pain. Jack is an extreme example. Over the course of several years, I'm able to piece together a history of trauma and foreboding that he played down or did not grasp for most of his life. He depicted his mother as devoted, adoring. For a long time, he told me, he was spoiled by her. When I questioned him about a "laziness" in his tone, a sagging quality, he connected it to expecting things to come to him. He could lay back and be adorable without having to lift a finger. Yet he exerted himself. He was a decent research scientist, tried to be a good father — failures bothered him. He worked at living. His sense that life would take care of him was more a fantasy than the way he lived, but it affected the texture and tone of his personality.

I could feel pockets of semicollapse like whirlpools yet somehow stagnant within larger areas of collapse, pockets organized by bitter self-pity, rage. I tell Jack what I see, and he says, "I'm a scientist and being a scientist has advantages. A scientist is interested in many things." He seems to be saying he can turn a scientific eye on his bitterness, self-pity, rage, collapse, and larger, more consuming panicky depression. The bitter self-pity is characterological, the depression-anxiety is something happening to his character.

Yet he has not scientifically put together a picture of his life that brings out forces that may be working. His life moves along beyond his capacity to see and feel it. Not seeing and feeling it enabled him to go through it fairly decently, up to a point. His breakdown challenges and overwhelms his science. The mind/life that wants to study itself is breaking down as it studies.

I'm able to say what he tells me. "You tell me your father had a heart attack when you were twelve. Your mother cared for him, then broke down. By the time you were thirteen, she went insane and had to be in a hospital. You took care of your parents with help. You visited her and brought her home. You saw her madness wax and wane. You tried to help her at home. Finally, she needed to live out her life in a hospital, where she died. You visited her in your adolescence, your youth, then as a man. You visited her in the hospital until she died."

His brother and his brother's daughter also went mad.

"Can you imagine what impact a father's heart attack, a mother's madness must have on a boy becoming a teenager?" I coach.

I wonder if he felt he caused his father's heart problem, his mother's insanity, if guilt was a factor driving him mad. Aside from imaginary causality, the bare impact of those who support him disintegrating must tear his insides out. Of course, he mobilized himself in the face of being torn.

Jack's life had many pleasures before depression and suicide threatened them. He held out a long time. He knew the joys of sex and study, the depths of family life. Full-blown depression-anxiety obliterate these joys. So much so that he and I begin to wonder if ever he knew joy. Pleasures yes, but joy?

"I didn't feel the pain of what happened to me," Jack says. "I went through it but didn't feel it. I did what I needed to and kept on doing it. I didn't feel anything about it. I didn't feel my feelings." This is one thing Jack says when I ask him repeatedly how he feels or felt or imagines he must have felt in the face of so much trauma. Trauma isn't traumatic when it just happens and you have to deal with it. Jack convinced himself he did not feel anything about it at all, that he faced life's difficulties and coped. He got from life what it offered or what he could. One scales down, puts effort into what's possible.

"Maybe it's a gene, a disease gene, a sick gene, and I held out as long as I could. I don't believe that explains it all. But I don't really feel what sounds like tragedy when you say it. It must affect, me but I really didn't and don't feel much about it . . ."—father's illness, mother's illness, brother's illness, niece's illness.

Jack held out as long as he could. Milton held out as long as he could. What is this holding out? Holding out for father to come? For mother to heal? For life to be over? For self to heal? For therapy to come? For God to come? To hold out and hold the course. We speak of people on strike as holdouts. A certain strength is necessary. What does one do with weakness?

"The only tear I really felt was moving when I was seven and having to leave the woman who took care of me. I still feel her soft skin on my cheek. I don't remember the feel of my mother's skin." This is the preeminent pain of childhood that Jack remembers. Otherwise, he feels he had a pretty decent childhood, playing with kids, a doting mother, a hard-working and loving father, a wonderfully soft and caring housekeeper, lots of fun things for a kid to do. He grew up in the country — swimming, fishing, running around. Then he was moved to the city, ripped from the warmth of his caretaker and his first seven years.

He made a go of it as a city boy. Oddly, he does not remember the toughness of city streets, fights, dangers, as painful. He adapts, does what he has to, stoic, able. He finds pleasures, things to do. The pain is for parting, the actual tearing away, leaving his early life and caretaker behind. He gets along well in his new life. He finds opportunities.

He does not miss the softness of his caretaker's skin or touch much until we talk about it. It comes back to him when he thinks of his mother trying to staple together a tear in his cheek when he ripped it playing. (She used a staple gun, as a doctor might, but without anesthesia. Perhaps she was being practical, but Jack is hinting of an apprehension of his mother's incipient madness long before the storm broke, latent madness fused with mother love.) His mother's touch comes back as causing pain, trying to patch a wound together. He contrasts it with his caretaker's soft skin against his cheek.

"I hear what you're trying to tell me. I push it away, wipe it out. I hear it in what I tell you. I try to be more in it. I hear myself speak about a wound, a rip, tear, pain with my mother, softness with a woman whose face I can't remember. I remember my mother's face, not touch. I remember my caretaker's touch, not face. I can't stay with trauma. I keep it away, hard to feel."

Jack nearly lost the capacity for joy. The only remaining moments of light I hear him mention have to do with his grandson. His grandson's smile, touch, presence light Jack's heart. Light kindles light for a time. Time spent with his grandson leaves a residue, even in the horror of depression. Other than this, he says his life is joyless. His grandson's light barely keeps him alive.

I feel he has been this way for years, making do, getting through, with waning flickers of interest.

He tells me he's going to kill himself, jump off a bridge, a building. I say I'll jump with him, we'll fall and hit water or ground together. He says over and over, "You're brave. You're brave. If I were you, I'd lock me away."

"You'd have to come out, sooner or later," I say. I don't feel brave. I feel *him*.

I feel our difference. I have deadness and depression, too — but also wings, loves, joys. What happened to his wings?

He claims his soul never was very alive. Collapse substitutes for soul life. Collapse and more collapse. He is already falling. He does not need to jump off a building or bridge to fall.

He tells me of an interview with a magician he saw on TV. Every winter the magician's parents took him south, and he never saw snow. He so wanted to see snow. One winter he convinced his parents to stay north and he got his heart's desire. Snowflakes.

Jack relishes this story. Somehow life wins out. A boy speaks up and is listened to. Jack says more about the snowflakes, the wonder, tingling beauty. He pictures beauty in his mind, not able to feel it in his body. He admires the boy's tenacity, life-feeling, awe, sparkling hope. He knows the boy is right: snowflakes are true.

Already blood begins to stain Jack's snow, but he sees the snowflakes falling. Still falling.

"Snowflakes," I say. "There's always snowflakes."

Jack: "They're always there?"

Me: "There's nothing else."

Jack: "That's true."

Fame must help some people, make them feel more expansive, more whole. But there is also what I call the "Jim Henson complex" — partly my fancy, perhaps not entirely. I think of Jim Henson getting sick and dying when he was selling Kermit the Frog to Disney.

My guess is Kermit played an important role in Jim Henson's psyche.

Kermit was his first successful Muppet, a breakthrough. Kermit (with Ernie in *Sesame Street*) became a central self figure, a core fictional voice that carried important identity feelings. The fact that Henson's world expanded to the point where he could consider selling rights to his old friend and alter-ego suggests the latter occupied less space in his psyche than it used to.

A variant of this alteration in self-feeling is akin to Bion's depiction of surgical shock, bleeding to death in your own vessels as a result of expansion of the latter, where emotional "space" is so vast a feeling can't be felt. I saw this happen dramatically in an encounter-sensitivity training group in the 1960s, when a lady insisted no one could hear her, that she could not hear herself. The group leader encouraged her to speak or scream as loudly as possible and she did. Still, she could not feel that she was audible, akin to some people scarcely feeling visible. Everyone felt she was quite loud, but as far as she was concerned, she might as well be yelling in a soundproof room. She couldn't feel anyone hearing her. She couldn't hear herself being heard. Her affective voice simply didn't feel its own impact.

Jim Henson's world expanded enormously, perhaps too greatly, so that he couldn't feel himself in a way. Of course, he enjoyed the expanded him, the fuller him. Of course, he may have remained just plain him too. But something of the pinch was lost, the smaller space that holds one. One starts with a hunger, rawness, longing that hits against a space one wishes were larger, although its smallness is soothing.

I read somewhere that Tennessee Williams complained he couldn't feel the sting or bite he once had, so he would travel in Mexico without money to try to recreate the feeling (unsuccessfully). My fancy is that Jim Henson's space expanded so much that he was in danger of not being able to feel himself in a way he once could. His psychesoma filled physical space (his lungs) in mistaken substitute for the emotional space that required compression (he drowned in his own lungs). Instead of too much room to breathe, too little. (I'm aware I'm creating a psychic visionary fiction about a physical illness).

There are ecstasies of fame. One imagines one will be more whole or powerful or recognized or acceptable when one is famous — and this may work in certain ways. But there is danger in thinning out, the higher one goes. Affective intensity may thin and become more diffuse as space grows, to the point where core self-feeling begins to fade. Or has to rev itself up so much to fill expanding space that it becomes unmanageable or unbearable.

Aliveness kills. Control of aliveness kills too.

My visionary fiction continues, although it is based on conviction formed by real events.

Most people who become famous or achieve new peaks of living may do well. But there are those who die or become ill upon achieving fame or upon breaking through personal barriers. This happens too often to be negligible.

A man's first book comes out, another man finally marries after years of loneliness, another's depression gives way to ecstasy — all accidentally drown. A man bent on pushing through personal limits dies in a mountain climbing fall, another falls off a cliff after his art begins to sell. A young pianist dies of cancer after a song he writes hits the charts. Another pianist, very like him, controlled, meticulous, cerebral contracts cancer after beginning his first sexual relationship. Car accidents, strokes, heart attacks, jumping off buildings — I've heard of these and more following a peak experience. In a variation, I read about an author of a best-seller killing himself a few years after his dog died. Would he have killed himself in despair over his dog before he became famous?

In everyday life people associate death or illness with traumatic events: a mother not recovering from a child's death, a husband falling ill after his wife dies, depression or illness following loss of love or money, and so on. One usually does not associate trauma with joy or ecstasy or intensely positive emotion.

A girl and I were kissing, and I felt more and more overwhelmed by joy. I *thought* I was going to pass out and die. I *felt* I was going to die. Of course, I *knew* I wasn't dying. It was just so good, so intense, so full. Overflowing fountains of feeling, never-ending, more and more.

Elizabethan poets knew these feelings well, loving-orgasm-dying. They sang them repeatedly, prolonging pleasure and joy into ever greater ecstasies-sorrows. Mixtures of abundance and grief, associations as old as experience. We draw them, dance them, think them, story them. Yet some people do die from them.

Ancient stories associate death and petrifaction with positive and negative extremes. See God or Medusa and die or turn to stone. Aaron's sons burn to a crisp trying to get too close to God the wrong way. If one looks back at destruction, one turns into a pillar of salt. If one looks back at beauty, one loses the loved one. If one approaches too much, too quickly—ouch!

Yet one *must* see God and Medusa. One must look back. One must approach with urgency. Extremes of experience are necessary. One wants to experience all one can, use one's equipment to the utmost. Extremes yield the greatest yum.

Do the ancient stories suggest a matter of dosage, ethics, aesthetics? Mosaic laws provide a filter, an ethics of approach-avoidance. Greek temples are another kind of filter, through architectural aesthetics. Jackson Pollock and Jack Kerouac were mad filters in my day, more like Aaron's sons, storming the gates without protection.

Many ancients advise a Middle Way. Freud writes that every psychic act is a compromise between forces. Multiple tensions feed every act. D. W. Winnicott, who wrote appreciatively of relatively tension free times, hungered for extremes, valued maximal aliveness. We thrive on both maximum aliveness and moments between.

Without extremes what would Middle be like? The latter feeds on the far sides.

Extremes and Middle are not at war. Neither exists without the other.

Extremes and Middle are at war. That is part of the way they exist together.

The soul pours everything into God. All aspirations, wishes for perfection, the end of disjunctions. In mystical contemplation God is conceived as a supramaximum—an amazing unity. "Hear, O Israel, the Lord is God, and God is One."

Here-hear. Presence, omnipresence. "I am the living God. I am where I am, will be where I will be. I will be there."

Go there—to the ends of space, to the core of earth, blow up bits of matter and imagine smaller bits to blow up. Under rocks, in heavens. God says, "Go wherever you will go; I will be there."

A matter of hearing/here-ing. "I will be where you are."

God, the greatest idol?

We create unimaginable imageless perfection, a One uniting everything in His/Her/Its being. Being-knowing are one. Mystical tradition tells us, He is in everything, knows everything, is everything. Permeates every pore. Omnipresence-omniscience-omnipotence—all, one, unity, totality. Absolutely! Totally!

And we taste this unimaginable, unthinkable One.

And now we conceive an evolutionary God, open, dynamic, ever changing, the God of every new moment, a God of new life, new spirit, a God of unique instants.

How can change be part of God if change makes God less perfect, if perfection is changeless?

Our sensibility is in love with change, so our God is a God of change.

Moments are our homes.

To love with one's whole heart—no greater passionate calling. "Love God with all your heart and all your soul and all your might."

This call is part of "Hear, O Israel."

It is an invitation, a plea, a request, a demand, a commandment (the first commandment). God asks us to love Him with all we are, with all our being. He does not ask whether or not we can. He tells us, love with everything you are, all your heart and soul and might and mind. All.

Sages give many interpretations, tell us that the ventricles of the heart symbolize higher-lower nature. No part of the heart is exempt from the first commandment, the first principle. Eastern sages write of right and left hearts. Everything is brought into the love striving. Our evil inclination is part of the mix, part of the *all*.

Strive to love with all your heart and soul and might.

The call ignites striving, grows out of tasting the great striving. A striving that gathers power, attracting other strivings into its orbit or current, yet leaves room for dissidence. A striving that feeds on fighting and surrender.

An *all* that makes one feel what life can be.

Torment is on every page of the Bible. High points of ecstasy—peaks of experience—run through torment. They refer to each other, pour through each other, make each other possible.

Biblical fever and fury are echoed in Shakespeare. Self and state replace God and Israel.

Torment seems to be ecstasy's filter and vice versa.

There is not a page in the Bible that ought not strike every reader dumb with dread.

If one took a page of the Bible seriously, one could not lift a finger against one's brother or sister or oneself. One might not be able to lift a finger—period. Struck dumb with awe and terror. It is easy to see why lifting a finger or hand can shock one into enlightenment in Zen Buddhism.

Terror subsides. One recovers and becomes oneself again. Processes of injury, corruption, power, and bickering continue. Even trying to help others often causes harm. One throws oneself into life with all one's might. Dread swims in the background. The life drive takes over. A life drive bubbling with destructive energy.

Still, there is the God of creativity, the God who feels life is good. There is a Moses in us seeing God face to face, at the center of being. Still, Moses and Abraham spend a lot of time persuading God not to destroy. And even Moses had to hide his head to see God's backside passing by.

Is God like a child who knocks down his building blocks? Only the blocks are real lives, nations, people, you and me.

Terror never goes away. It is part of background restlessness. It fades into the pleasure of living, bony fins in the feeling of creative power.

We destroy each other with our ecstasies.

We uplift each other with our ecstasies.

Moses tries to cajole, argue, scare Israel into compliance. "You hear God's voice, see God's fire. You are there. You see and feel and hear God's presence. You are too afraid to stand it and make me a go-between for you."

Always a filter, a proxy, a substitute. Always face to face. Never quite face to face.

Warriors, slaughter. Follow the laws or else. If you don't, everything will boomerang. You will be afraid of your own shadow.

We are afraid of shadows.

Shakespeare portrays delusion, falling apart, torment, malice, the unkindness of humankind. Fever and infection are among his favorite images: "life's fitful fever," "your potent and infectious fevers."

"Better be dead . . . / Than on the torture of the mind to lie / In restless ecstasy."

But it is precisely this tormented ecstasy we live.

Today's the day (like every day) that things will go better. I wake up and slowly begin to feel good. I think about the difficulties of the day before and resolve to do better. Doesn't one learn a little from day to day?

I begin to wear down as the day goes on. Finally, a family outing does it. No one agrees on where to go when. Splits everywhichway. My younger boy rides off on his bike full speed away from the rest of us. He does not get his way, so he is determined we will not get ours. I suspect he has some kind of awareness that he is inflicting pain. I have no doubt he began experiencing a blinding pain of his own and, as it began to mount, deflected it by speeding off. Some of it lands in me.

My wife and older boy go on ahead of me. My bike goes slower and slower. I feel the mounting pain and imagine what it would be like to give in to it. If I totally gave in to it, I would have to stop riding, get off my bike, double over on the side of the path, fall into the bushes, lie quietly or thrash. A ball of pain. Slits up and down my insides and across my guts and chest. Knots within knots in the middle.

Morning bliss replaced by afternoon pain.

I keep riding and put a tracer on it.

I hang out with my older boy while he gets something to eat at a roadside stand. He spills gazpacho all over himself. A rather mild way of showing his mess or responding to mine. He's not in a bad mood.

It's me who's going down. Visions of all the many times I blamed a girlfriend for this bad feeling. So many times blaming someone, one of my kids, my wife, something at work. This black mood, soul-curdling. Ah, it's me, my own, mine. My bile, my muckyuck. It's not someone else's "fault" — this downspin, this infection.

I fight it somewhat while keeping part of an eye on it. Try to miniaturize or telescope or partly encapsulate it. Like a spider tying up a bug for later consumption. It's a black and red spiny ball that tastes bad, and I've got to work with it. Meanwhile, do anything but don't let it ruin my day, especially the day of those near me.

I become several people at once. I'm aware of more than one kind of activity going on in me at the same time. I'm contracting around the black-red pain ball, holding it for later, noticing transformations it undergoes, somewhat isolating myself, placing myself in an internal infirmary, protecting others from my noxious impact. At the same time I try to keep an open area for the day as it unfolds. How would things go if I were not in such a black state, if I were not so readily ruptured?

I fear my poison affects those around me no matter what. The reality is we are permeable and permeate each other. We nourish-poison each other moment to moment and across time. Perhaps the evil impact can be mitigated somewhat by talking. Everyone in the family catches up with each other, and we go over what happened without driving things into the ground. At least we talk it over a little, if not talk it out.

The day does not end badly. The kids kayak across the lake, swim and watch a comedy. My wife and I read and swim. I feel the black ball and some room around it. I see it's not her black ball. It's mine.

I come back from the lake without my glasses and go into a panic. All of a sudden it hits me that I can't see. What was I doing before I realized I didn't have my glasses on? So, one way or another, there are leaks. My kids and I play cards. I go to sleep early. I feel residuals of soul curdle. What am I learning? I'm learning it's part of *me*. It may or may not be part of others. But it certainly belongs to *me*.

My younger boy can't fall asleep. He comes in during the night for company.

No man is an island. Self impacts in all directions.

We keep learning, don't we?

Some people are better at night. I'm better in the morning. Like a flower that opens with the sunlight and closes with darkness.

My younger boy and I feel each other out in the morning, a little wary. Then things fall into a better groove than yesterday. We become happy and mellow.

Today we all agree on the bike ride we're taking.

For a few moments, at least, happiness is not a danger signal.

When I have time, I stare at the pain ball and watch it slowly rotate. I pull on it, open it like a fruit—red, black, blue strands. Poison fruit. Impacted wounds. Trauma before I can think or remember. All the hate of my childhood, the fear of life. The anguish never goes away. It can be set off in a moment—by a glance, a word.

I think of a girl who hurt my feelings, and in an instant I started coughing, instant bronchitis. I can get sick instantaneously from a bad word or glance. Not so much anymore. For many years I got sick from a moment's rejection without quite putting it together.

Gradually, the pain became more visible. The pain ball. I became ill less often.

There's something oddly strengthening about opening the pain, wading in, jumping in. Pulling the poison fruit around me, stickiness prickly and oozy. To some extent, pain means I'm somewhere where the Other isn't. Contact with it makes me stronger. It is something like a toothache for a compass point. You can sometimes find where you are by feeling it. By following the pain, you find where you are hiding.

If you follow the pain all the way, you pass through a barrier.

I discovered this accidentally one day when I was a young man and just terribly unhappy. It happened once on a bus. I doubled over in agony and went deeper and deeper into it. At some point there was a semiblackout and everything reversed, passing through a vaginal opening into heavenly sky. Stars. Light. Radiance.

The common saying about being hit so hard you see stars is dramatically true. Van Gogh's *Starry Night* comes to mind. I can scarcely imagine the agony he went through to make the ecstasy of the stars real.

It can happen in broad daylight. In college, one spring morning, I put Vivaldi on and threw open the window, and instantaneously, upon hearing the music and feeling the air and seeing the sunlight, agony subsided, replaced by joy. A joy burst. Thought disappeared. This moment of absolute joy felt more real and true than all the agony before it.

Seeing the stars for the first time when I was a little over two.

Hearing the clarinet played when I was seven or eight and I couldn't stop laughing.

Kissing Laurel good-night in high school.

Vivaldi and an open window one spring morning in college.

A tree in an abandoned lot in Twin Peaks in the late 1950s.

Inner heart-vagina opening to radiance in my twenties.

Radiant eyes and smiles of women in sexual intercourse.

Little by little, ecstatic moments, joy bursts, unite. The stream grows stronger, supports many subcurrents. One locates it in muted forms daily. Ever ready, it swirls through cracks of experience, licks crevices, twists and turns. Warmer, cooler, sunnier, darker.

Pain cements personality together. Joy also. Affects change nuances, tones, textures, colors. Seasoned hearts come through.

A conjugation:
>I'm mad that I'm mad.
>I'm sad that I'm mad.
>I'm glad that I'm mad.
>I'm sad that I'm sad.
>I'm glad that I'm sad.
>I'm sad that I'm glad.
>I'm glad that I'm glad.
>Zest
>— Clifford Scott

Basic sandwich: Glad-mad-sad-Glad.

Zest Sandwich. Ecstasy Sandwich.

At the Passover Seder we eat a Hillel sandwich: bitter herbs and charoset between matzos. Who knows what symbols mean? We make up meanings by searching ourselves and the vast unknown.

Bitter herbs = life's bitterness, the slave aspect of living. Passover is about slavery-freedom, closed-open, limited-infinite, bitterness-joy.

Charoset is a mixture of chopped fruit and nuts and wine. There are variations. The bitter is sweetened.

Charoset and bitter herbs may signify cement made to bind great pyramid rocks. Bitter herbs: *Maror* (Hebrew for bitter herbs) = mortar.

In unconscious logic: bitter is sweet and sweet is bitter. Experience is one.

There are infinite dimensions in unconscious logic: while sweet and bitter are one, each signifies the other in acts of reversal. One is the other. One becomes the other. One signifies or substitutes for the other. One refers to the other as they co-constitute one another. One is not the other. For example, love-hate fuse, substitute for each other, undergo reversals, oppose each other, enter variations of separation-union.

Sarah's bitter laugh mocks God's promise that she will bear fruit in old age. Naomi is bitter (with cause), but Ruth follows her. The bitter thread keeps one real, keeps one in touch with injury. Bitter trauma. Sarah "eats" her bitter laugh, names her fruit "Yitzchak" (Isaac), "Laughter." Freud notes the binding of injury with laughter in jokes.

We eat the bitterness that cements personality together. By eating, we assimilate it. It becomes part of us and we transcend it. I am and am not my bitterness. We are and are not our bitterness. Bittersweet cement.

Sentimental bittersweet — pale reflection of Sarah's laugh.

You probably know Hillel's famous saying, "If I'm not for myself, who will be for me? If I'm only for myself, what am I? If not now, when?" Or his reply when asked to give the essence of Torah while standing on one foot–"Do not do to others what you don't want them to do to you." Hillel tries to balance forces, the movement toward self, toward other, a mixture of dignity, receptivity, caring, urgency. The point of a sandwich is to mix, to bring together, to make a selection that works.

Matzah is unleavened bread, bread that does not rise, humility, non-ego, faith, spiritual "poverty"—not being puffed up. Hillel's sandwich keeps things in perspective. Yet, ah! the sweetness, the deep, deep joy.

Not simply joy deeper than bitterness but altogether mixed. My father took delight in impressing me with the image of Hebrew slave's blood mixed in mortar, red of wine, soul of blood. Abhorrent delight mixed in blood of cement.

A sandwich seems so hierarchical. A faith sandwich, bittersweet. Bitter joy.

Trauma seems manageable by symbols, stories, images. But what about Sarah dying when Abraham takes Yitzchak to the sacrificial altar—laughter dies heartbroken. A story too? How can we take the real thing?

The morning prayers include a passage from Exodus detailing mixing spices for incense. The mix includes "galbanum," which has a foul odor. Spices of varied scents and functions are fully mixed. There is an area of the soul in which all experiences are so well mixed they create a unique scent not reducible to any one of them.

Abraham's test is Sarah's death.
Is the God who passes Abraham against woman's laughter?
Are Sarah and Abraham pounded together in the incense cup?

And the Ecstasy Sandwich? Glad-mad-sad-Glad? No sandwich at all—all mixed? Affect is psychic blood, the soul that's in the blood.

One story says mad is earlier than sad. I'd rather be mad than sad. As I grow, I allow more sad and feel for others as myself. Sometimes I feel sad about being mad. Even sad about being glad.

Sometimes glad leaves others out. It can leave me out too. How can glad leave everyone out?

A feeling can be so big there's no room for anything else. Glad takes over, swells, intoxicates. Before I know it, there is little room for me—or anyone. Glad fills all the space.

Sad about glad makes room for people.

Sad or mad can be bad too and leave out everything but itself. Feelings swell like bee stings and consume attention. Some people are allergic to such stings and can be in danger of dying.

It takes growth or a good mixture of spices to reach "I'm glad I'm glad" in such a way that sad and mad are absorbed in the mix, not cast out. All emotions are parts of each other, with room for variable, mutually qualifying play. Trauma sandwiches, joy sandwiches — pounded together in the spice cup. Part of the mix.

I place mad-sad between glads. Not always possible.

Glad sometimes goes to extremes to be a container. Rabbi Akivah was so in love with God he hoped God would give him a chance to die as a martyr with God on his lips. He loved God with all his heart and soul and might. As the Romans skinned him, his soul and mouth watered the world with God's presence.

Rabbi Akivah learned to read Hebrew in his forties and became a great Torah man. He became Torah and Torah became him. He became part of the flame that burns in us, that we fear will burn us, without which we are hollow.

"Man does not live by bread only, but by everything that proceeds out of the mouth of God."

Rabbi Akivah hungered for *this* everything!

His memory makes us feel this everything.

Another Rabbi Akivah story. Three great men enter paradise. One goes mad, one commits suicide. Rabbi Akivah returns renewed and refreshed.

I visited Rabbi Akivah's grave in Israel. Was he really buried there? A presence hovers and uplifts. Spiritual presences are more or less concentrated in different places.

Rabbi Akivah's imprint is etched more deeply on my soul because I visited his grave. My soul has a marker, like letters on a tombstone: Rabbi Akivah. Nothing remarkable about Akivah's grave site except spirit in sunlight.

I think of the story of a glow coming from the shul where an illiterate boy, knowing nothing but letters from the alphabet, was saying, "Aleph, Bet, Gimmel . . ." He said these letters with all his love.

Hebrew letters are mixtures of flames and tears.

They contain, too, male and female elements, generative elements, sperm and ova.

They evolved a long way from the first numinous lines and spaces, less wriggly, more stylized, massive, unyielding. But they still are strongly evocative. They contain many evocations of divinity.

So much can be encoded in a small space on a computer chip. But that is nothing compared with what can shimmer in micromoments of soul.

Akivah's spirit shimmers.

How can a soul shine more brightly as the body's skin is peeled?

Skinless body, skinless soul.

When I met with W. R. Bion in New York, I told him I found him joyless.

He had a knack of considering something yet responding nearly immediately — a kind of reflective immediacy.

He almost instantaneously said something like, "Then you must realize joy in your body, all through you. It must shine in your skin." He was telling me that if joy was important to me, it should pervade my being and be incarnate. Not just a vision — not visionary joy. If feeling is real, body lives it. It must shine in the skin and pores and muscles and senses. Not only in the mind. Not just sensation or thought of joy.

I thought of Rilke, Keats, the conjunction of joy and beauty, although Rilke's joy seemed to lack humor.

Bion and I spoke of many things in a fairly short time. I noticed that he was not in a hurry to end our sessions. We drifted on, and I, finally, feeling guilty, would begin to go. That is my nature. I break contact too quickly. I think of the way he stood there waiting for me, chatting on, whenever I ended a session quickly. He left time open for a slow ending or continuation.

To be able to wait for each other — such a valuable trait. How many of us can do this or want to most of the time?

His seminar that I attended had many difficult moments. There were very "bright" analysts in the group who were used to a certain kind of intellectual fare, and Bion did not fit the mold. Frustration was palpable, ever hovering near sarcasm and stings that brightness makes too easy. Yet there were members who worked hard and shared difficulties. Barriers were struggled with, and we began digging. Tensions that come with staying with the thing at hand mounted. We gravitated toward blocks that mark sessions and destructive areas of self. When the evening neared its end, relief began to feel palpable and more than relief—a certain joy at coming through something. I imagined Bion looked at me a moment when he remarked, "Yes and how odd to feel such joy at working so hard with these difficulties."

I don't recall his exact words, but there was appreciation of joy that comes from sticking with blocks of self wherever they lead. Staying and staying with what needs staying with. Psychoanalytic joy, a grueling kind of joy. Very real nonetheless, bottom-up joy making its way through the work itself.

The Omaha Beach landing scene, in Steven Spielberg's movie *Saving Private Ryan* depicts horrible moments with reverberations beyond literal horror. American soldiers in landing barges were decimated by German guns. Many could not begin to disembark. They were blown away as barge doors opened.

It seemed almost a matter of numbers, more American bodies attempting to land than German bullets able to keep up with them. More bodies than bullets.

Wave after wave of soldiers landing, getting slaughtered—depicted in ghastly detail. Yet soldiers began to get through, to establish beachheads, to develop positions, and gradually prevail. Bodies everywhere. Slaughter and sacrifice.

There was virtually no chance that the first to try to land could survive. Yet there had to be the first and second and third waves. There had to be enough waves of bodies for the job to get done, enough live bodies to thread through the dead.

Human beings like ants. You keep crushing the ants, and still there are more that keep coming.

Which live, which die?

Sacrificial slaughter. Some get through. Enough get through.

Generational waves. We keep coming, building, reshaping. Incessantly.

The movie spans the horror and the triumph. Mass and random slaughter is steadfast. Death is an anchor, whether it comes quickly or slowly. Bodies blown open, insides gushing out is a constant in the movie's depiction of reality. If you can't deal with bodily insides in your face, you deal with nothing.

In one scene a dying soldier tries to tuck his guts in. I understand that he was trying to live in the face of disbelief. But I could not help feeling — perhaps my idiosyncrasy — he was being modest. He was trying to tuck himself in before dying. A little like covering nakedness or closing an opening (our need to close a corpse's mouth). An act of modesty and dignity before death. Modesty and dignity belong together.

Life keeps emerging.

The movie ends with a sense of goodness coming through. Evil is uncompromised and uncompromising. Goodness may be fragile, ineffable, but no less real. More real, perhaps. Is it only sentimentality — Hollywood, after all — that goodness is more true, more real than very true and real evil?

A compelling case for goodness is made because evil is not obscured by it. Goodness does not blot out evil or substitute for it or escape it.

Images of war run through Bion's depictions of therapy sessions. Fear is the dominant emotion in battle. Fear and fury.

Yet many soldiers speak of the pleasures of battle. Can that be?

I've heard men say they were never more alive than in battle. Life's greatest intensity — ordinary life pales by comparison.

Look at Homer's depiction of war, its glories and insanities.

Glory.

Hidden ecstasies in war? Not so hidden?

Pride of battle?

I don't think ecstasy was Spielberg's dominant tone. Beside fear, slaughter, sacrifice was a sense that people were getting a job done. They did what they had to and then some. They found ways to do the work.

The work is the arena for emotional flow or frozenness. Intensity, blankness. ingenuity, luck, disappearance, regrouping, persistence. Individuals are wasted or get through but groups go on — more individuals pick up the slack.

Bion never stopped saying that fear was his dominant feeling in battle. He was decorated as a hero but insisted he was a coward.

Where is the ecstasy of slaughter? So many movies delight in plunder, rape, dominance-submission, intrigues of war. Spielberg depicts the fear, the job, the work, the requirements, the madness, and, sentimental or not, he says something more: not all the evils in life can nullify the good thread.

In the Second World War, Bion worked as an army psychiatrist treating battle-shocked soldiers (in the First World War he had been a tank commander). His job was to get soldiers back to battle as soon as possible. He worked with groups.

He depicts groups as a kind of war zone, the therapist as shocked as anyone. Even at the end of his life, Bion depicts the therapist as trying to think while under fire. Shock describes emotional impact, intensity of feeling. Emotional waves = shock waves.

What if one is too scared to feel? Numbed by shock. Maximum and minimum emotion become each other. Heightened intensity = the null dimension. Too much becomes too little, and the system shuts off. Violence and blankness.

Bion's depictions of groups can be Pinteresque. The play begins with the therapist alone on stage, spotlight on him. Perhaps he feels decent if things are good for him, an ordinary benevolent baseline. Enter the patients. They begin to sit, talk. Pressures build. The therapist undergoes disturbances and deformations. Patients try to push someone (one another, the therapist) into doing work that needs to be done. Evasion rampant.

What work? Quite simply, to restore the capacity to feel. To become a feeling self. Particularly, a feeling self under pressures not to feel.

There are scenes in *Saving Private Ryan* when sound stops. Action continues. This happens because of the deafening effects of gunfire. But it also expresses states of shock. Functioning is put on hold. A kind of mental blackout. One is gone. One sees bodies and activity going on but is temporarily paralyzed. A frozen zone.

The point of therapy is to enable the sound to come back on, to thaw out.

A lifelong process.

What is happening between you and me, every you and me?

Spielberg said he drew a line beyond which he would not go. He would not depict all the horrors, only horror up to a point. A certain modesty before horror?

I don't think accounts of therapy can depict the mixtures of horror and goodness that pervade sessions. Some try, up to a point.

Would the public be horrified to know how numbed therapists can be? More than battle "fatigue." Therapists can be put out of play — often without knowing it — by the impact of emotional events they cannot keep up with or decipher.

Therapy is as much for the therapist as for the patient. A therapist uses therapy to evolve equipment to do therapy. One tries to let oneself think and feel as therapy is going on. A lot of therapy work goes on unconsciously between meetings. One comes to the next meeting with work needed the meeting before.

There are difficulties that prevent one from being in the session one is in at the moment. Partly because processes in time are ahead of and behind themselves.

Part of the ecstasy-dread of therapy is awareness that the work itself is a difficulty threaded over time. The patient, after all, is in the same boat. Neither therapist nor patient may *know* what is happening at a given time, but either or both may have a *sense* of it. *Sensing this sense* and speaking from it builds the ability to do so again.

Two people together may be more or less in shock at the same time. Therapy provides experience in sensing this shock, feeling it, sometimes speaking from it (one's own voice in the whirlwind).

Does one only get from therapy an ability to do therapy? Can one use therapy to access other dreads-ecstasies? Can one use therapy to step out of therapy?

Therapists often say that they are most alive and real while doing therapy. Therapy becomes a way of life and life a form of therapy.

Is that an argument against it?

Once addicted to therapeutic ecstasy is one fit for the front line?

Does an ecstatic therapist lose her or his warrior edge?

Judging from wars that go on between therapists, never fear.

War is a constant as fields shift.

If numbness, violence, and ecstasy are connected, what can one do?

In therapy ones tries to stay with these connections and stay with them some more. If one stays with something, something happens.

Somewhere William Blake writes about heaven as a war between all voices maximally expressing themselves, benefiting all. In heaven no conflict is compromised. Absolute conflict brings absolute reward. That is probably because all conflicts are mediated through imaginative expression.

Shakespeare makes the most of the oneness of experiencing. Opposites merge. Confusion reigns. Rational distinctions float on depths of madness, idiocy, scathing passion. Reality is beautiful-horrifying-mad.

Romantic love is a "fever," an "uncertain sickly appetite."

"Desire is death."

One is "frantic-mad with evermore unrest"; one's love is "black as hell, as dark as night."

This is ecstatic suffering.

A goal is to turn the tables, to "feed on Death" rather than be food for Death.

One becomes inwardly rich sucking on nipples of death-idiocy-madness and the ecstatic beauty that permeates "uncertain sickly appetite."

One turns the tables by feeling what there is to feel.

One turns the tables with poems and plays.

Experience is civil war.

Foul-fair mixed, reversed, impossible to keep straight: opposites pollute, reciprocal contamination the rule.

Shakespeare offers a meditation on death, lunacy, vanity, confusion, fury, fever, the dementia of living.

One turns the tables by being alive and noticing.

"Within be fed . . . So shalt thou feed on Death."

To meditate on the object of desire as black as hell and desire as death digs deep wells in self. One follows the thread of desire and hell and death deeper than any imaginable maze. Mazes invaginate life's surface. One takes many paths at once, torn by them all.

Desire, death, hell drive one deeper, no matter what the path.

Shakespeare points to a deranged X that ruins living as it heightens it.

To some extent, acts of creative imagination are salvific. One can envision horror and lunacy, feel it deeply, create and document it, be nourished by the gruesome irony that beauty breeds on horror. Beauty-horror breed one another. A creative act is its own justification. Creative acts are time capsules unique in every living present, growing in the soil of time and ever in eternity.

Is reading Shakespeare redemptive?

Deep alchemy at work, emotional chemistry.

Yes, Shakespeare wrote and acted and put on plays and invested in real estate to make money. He was realistic. He made his living, he made his way.

Perhaps he started by rewriting other people's work. When did Shakespeare become Shakespeare? When did the writing take on a life of its own, mine the deep veins, take wing, become a propulsive force—words more real than trees and stars, characters more real than people? How did living on the surface turn life inside out?

Black love, black desire, black death: pages stamped with madness and nullity, beauty runs through them. Shining madness, luminous death, sickly decay. Rot—states, selves, bodies. The signature of death-life: death and life filtered through each other on every page.

Secularized biblical intensity, the anguished voice of living moving from peak to peak.

Like the Bible, the work is unflinching. It doesn't deviate. It gets the "feel" of the human condition in every molecular word. It turns the prism slightly, beams in. Dark diamonds. Flesh sound and rant and calling out: nothing to nowhere.

Who is Shakespeare talking to? Not just high-low groups of his time or to us now. He is anguish talking to emptiness. Emotional intensity speaking on the edge of stupor, a commanding and pleading void in the fullness of space-time. Sometimes a creative act speeds away from its center with frightening velocity, all the more eerie and compelling because so much weight is weightless.

David, the psalmist, moves us because he speaks to God. A longing heart cries out. We never hear God speaking to him. We hear God in David's outcry.

God moves inexorably but with the possibility that any moment His heart may open.

Some of us reach God some of the time. Hearts touch.

God and self keep moving. Self collapses, slips back, goes its way, reaches out again.

All hope is pinned on loose threads.

How can we feel so close to a Presence we can't see or hear or touch? Is invisibility, intangibility, inexistence a condition for ineffable closeness?

God, the Place.

Is storming God something like storming any enemy beach? Some of us get through, some prevail.

Animal sacrifice didn't work. Who knows how many hundreds or thousands of years people tried to purify themselves through animals.

The Bible describes sacrificial rites in detail. What sort of animal meets what sort of specifications for what sin. Who should do what when.

A central temple, a great temple.

Perhaps it was all too static.

I feel awe in every passage, trembling hopes, the wish to get it right.

Better animals than people.

Some people at certain times performed human sacrifices to purify themselves or gain power.

The need to purge, achieve catharsis, cleanse, assimilate power. To be spotless and powerful.

Stain of sin, corruption. Shakespeare's rot, vanity, madness, confusion, "restless ecstasy."

Follow your own eyes and heart — the sickness thereof. Follow your bliss — the madness thereof.

Power-mad brains and bodies leering at neighbor's goods.

A problem with original sin is its referring to Adam and Eve, a spot in time. The reverse is likely. Time is the spot, or the spot is the origin of time. Time, vitality, drive. The only way to rid oneself of stain is to cleanse the life drive. Shakespeare's paradoxical undercurrent: how can one be totally alive and purge oneself of the urge to exist? Only by cleansing the will to live can one rid oneself of life's poison.

Contrary to what once was popular belief, there are animals who kill each other for sport, fun, enjoyment of energy.

Is there anything docile about energy as such?

Can one channel it through animal sacrifice?

It was a brilliant try or hope — the attempt to divert aggression onto animals and away from people. Kill animals, not people. Let animals substitute for people as object of cleansing murder.

We could not cut sin out of us. We could not lift out the stain. We could not get rid of life and live. Let animals stand for sin and stain and get rid of the latter through them. Let the blood of animals wash our sin away. A stainless animal for our stained soul.

Cannibalism and sacrificial murder circulates around Jesus of Nazareth. The incorruptible one for our corruption. God's sacrifice for us rather than ours for God. It works both ways, two-way energy-sincerity flow. We sacrifice for one another. We sacrifice one another for ourselves.

New kinds of sacrifice: self-sacrifice, sacrificial dimension in spirit. Not bodies, souls.

The Prophets' contempt for substituting tithes or animals for work self must do. New twist! The great temple is gone. The temple is the soul, work all must do. Circumcision of the heart. Good deeds, caring for the needy — which is everyone's self. We are ministers of self everywhere. Not animal sacrifice, but sacrificial journey. Sacrifice as Mystery, gateway to ever new life.

Life as Opening.

To my knowledge, Shakespeare did not kill anyone. His plays are filled with murders, cries of agony. They strip skin away, bare soul's hysteria. Fevered words rather than brutal acts. Uplifting, menacing words, verbal knives that inspire and unmask. Theater and printed page rather than battlefield and backstreet.

Words peel minds away.

Bible, Buddha, Socrates, Shakespeare — mindpeelers. Let grisly stain and goodness shine. Let unraveling begin.

Violence seeks new homes. Terror does not confine itself to theater and print. Animals do not work. Theater does not work.

Nonviolence whets appetites it aims to subdue.

Murder is everywhere. The ecstatic, anguished cry of murder.

Every single human being who ever lived or will live is called on to trace the murderer to the bitter end. To trace self to the bitter end, to endlessness.

You and I are ecstatic, anguished murderers.

Follow the trail to the villain aliveness. The aliveness that makes us happy, the aliveness that makes us sad.

Murder is built into aliveness. Ecstasy covers it.

Ecstasy is built into aliveness. Murder covers it.

What *do* we do with aliveness?

Winnicott democratizes murder. Murder is part of everyday life. We destroy ourselves and each other constantly. We are always killing each other as part of the backdrop of unconscious fantasy. The urge to kill is part of every interaction.

It is not all we are, but we are not without it.

It can break in and ruin a good moment anytime — like a child's irritation or fit.

Funny term, "break." To break in like a criminal or break out like a plague. Breaking a hope or tie or person — a breakdown. Children are always being broken for breaking things.

One may say I'm sorry forever.

One may train oneself to be stoic and take it.

One may exult in the ability to be cruel, part of freedom.

One may learn to oscillate between peace and sword.

Winnicott's notion is something different. We need to evolve to the point where we can outlast, if not embrace, each other's destructive element. Destructiveness is part of aliveness. Winnicott feels it is crucial for a baby to have a sense that another can take his or her aliveness. When the destructiveness built in to aliveness and a vital part of self comes flying at the mother, can the mother not retaliate?

Not just a matter of turning the other cheek.

Not only a matter of delighting in baby's energy, although that can be part of it.

There is a moment when embracing baby's energy is not the point, but not retaliating is. At such a moment, the caregiver or caretaker (give-and-take) is not long-suffering or striking back or resentful. Everything hinges on recognizing the destructive "attack" for what it is, a spontaneous part of aliveness. The destructive momentum of aliveness is joined by a spontaneous act of recognition.

This does not mean the mother subjects herself to chronic injury. It does mean she does not blow up imaginary injury and respond in moralistic, annihilating ways. It involves human beings evolving to the point where they make room for the destructive element that is part of the backcloth of relationships. It means making room for disturbing feelings.

If we make room for each other we won't have to murder each other — at least, murder won't be lethal. We mitigate effects of murderous feelings by making room for them. We make room for ourselves and each other in such a way that murder will not be fatal. If we get it right, just the opposite. Murder feeds living. It is part of the rich stream of feeling that adds complexity and shading. Murder is part of the way we grow.

An ideal or optimal scenario might be the baby lashing out, all-out striving, perhaps in fury, a full blast explosion, and the mother absolutely delighting in the baby's energy. This can happen if the baby's distress doesn't dominate pleasure, if the mother isn't getting hurt, if the mother's joy outweighs fear or anger. A crucial element is baby's bursting out with all his might and the mother not collapsing (withdrawing, lashing out, turning off, etc.). The baby feels there is room for himself and his energy in existence. And there is room for the other. Neither self nor other gets destroyed. The mother survives, perhaps delights in, the onslaught.

"Energy is Eternal delight."

Affirmation of self and energy would be enough, but Winnicott goes further. The result of the mother's survival is the birth or renewal of a sense of otherness. The other's essential self does not undergo alteration for the worse as a result of my attacks. The result may be expressed something like the following: "I do not damage or do in the other by my energic display. My energy does not warp or stain or poison or mar or spoil the other. The other can manage or take or survive me without collapse or loss of integrity. My life and might and all-out destructiveness does not destroy. The other is more than the sum of my destructiveness. The other can take my joy."

The advent of the sort of other that can take me makes it possible to use the other for growth purposes. If I do not have to spend much time worrying about how I'm affecting the other, I can use the other's not-me material for psychic growth. An important aspect of existence is launched and validated:

    1. We use each other for mutual growth.

    2. We survive each other's mutual use.

    3. We ruthlessly take what we need from each other's insides.

    4. We all gain from the taking.

Eating God is a good model for part of what we need to do with each other.

Joy and mutual appreciation become as necessary and natural as food.

A Utopian vision — perhaps?

Partly reworking Freud's life and death drives, Winnicott drops the death drive as primary but makes active destructive energy part of aliveness, part of what gives Eros thrill and verve. Without it, psychophysical life is flabby and flat.

Fearful or realistic argument: if a baby's destructive force is affirmed, won't that make the baby unrealistic and give her a sense that she can do anything she pleases, get away with everything? Won't that make her feel as if she can run over everyone to get her way? Won't she feel that only *her* energy counts, the other exists mainly to support her? Won't that make her a *user* in the negative sense: she will just *use* people?

Isn't this shallow and abusive? Will she be a baby all her life?

Winnicott feels there is a time when it is good for the mother to adapt to the baby's needs. A natural rhythm develops between greater-lesser adaptiveness. There will be times when mother is more attuned to baby and others when she is more focused on herself. Natural imbalances occur in both directions.

It is ghastly to deprive an infant of the moment's necessary adaptation out of fear the moment will last forever. It is good to have such moments in one's soul and good they last forever. It gives one faith that one is worth adapting to, one's life is worth the bother.

Winnicott also describes the interplay of illusion-disillusion. For example, the illusion of being the center of the universe enters corrective rhythm with the discovery that one is not. Both poles contribute to richness of living. The sense of being a (not the) center of being can fuel life for good.

I think of the story of a guru who tells his disciple to keep thinking, "I am God, I am God." Years later the teacher sees his student lame and bandaged. "What happened? What went wrong?" The disciple replies, "A man on an elephant refused to move off my path. 'I am God, I am God,' I kept thinking. And he ran over me." "Fool," the wise man said. "He's God too."

A sense of the holiness of self includes all selves.

Nearly total adaptation to a baby is possible in part because the baby does not have an adult body. It is not big enough to do the harm grownups can.

This is a little like Freud's picture of dreamlife. We can have violent and sexual encounters in dreams because it is safe to do so. Our bodies are lying safely in bed.

If we were totally grown up babies or dominated by dream processes while awake, the world would be in even worse trouble than it is.

The fact we are partly grown up babies and partly dominated by dream-work (more than we imagine) partly accounts for some of our troubles and joys.

It is wrong to think that being babies and dreamers causes our difficulties. But it is equally wrong to think infantile processes and dreaming (nightmares) don't magnify, inflate, exacerbate them. We will never free ourselves from infancy and dreams, nor is it necessarily desirable to do so. The job is more along the line of becoming better partners with our various selves, psychosocial-psychospiritual midwifery as long as we go on.

Winnicott's vision presents a truth and a challenge. In fact, we can and do adapt to one another all life long. And there are moments of need when such adaptation can be more whole and total than at other times. We give this to each other. We expect it. Some call it empathy or understanding or caring or love or compassion. We feed each other with whatever wisdom is part of us. If we live deeply and openly enough, with luck, wisdom grows.

The adaptation a mother provides a baby's energic might is something we give ourselves and one another throughout our lives. It is something we are always learning to do. It provides a basis for mutual appreciation.

People who taste this deep give-and-take can't get enough of it. Beating one another to a pulp fades as a compelling interest or drive. The drive to dominate and exercise power becomes part of a more mysterious and compelling need—to open and keep opening. This mysterious and compelling need, I believe, is the most satisfying drive of all: to be with oneself and others in ways that nourish living, that yield abundant life. Our destructiveness and murder—never gone—become part of a larger mix, subcurrents contributing to ecstatic energy that includes all centers of being.

The medieval saying that God is a circle whose center is everywhere and whose circumference is nowhere is true for all sentient beings, consciousness, precious life forms.

"For every thing that lives is holy."

Utopian vision — perhaps. Once one begins tasting it, nothing is more real.

A little Blakefest:

"He who sees the Infinite in all things sees God. He who sees the Ratio only, sees himself only."

"Exuberance is Beauty"

"Man has no Body distinct from his Soul for that called Body is a portion of Soul discerned by the five Senses, the chief inlets of Soul in this age."

"Energy is the only life and is from the Body and Reason is the bound or outward circumference of Energy."

"Energy is Eternal Delight."

"Excess of sorrow laughs. Excess of joy weeps."

"Joys impregnate. Sorrows bring forth."

"My senses discovered the infinite in everything."

"If the doors of perception were cleansed everything would appear to man as it is: infinite."

"For every thing that lives is Holy."

Could Blake have made this last statement if he had seen the melting flesh and freaks of Hiroshima, the emaciated survivors of the Holocaust, the racial and territorial brutalities that mock earth today?

His message would have been even more intense.

He would have depicted ripped and melted flesh, misshapen bodies, horrors of weaponry with the same wrath reserved for black lungs of children or religious and political bigotries (in which murder of spirits-bodies go together).

He battled constriction of Vision. Suffocating worldviews feed death and torture. Enlargement of Vision vs. Enlargement of Destruction. Useful knowledge can be part of either.

War involves territory, what is mine (ours) vs. what is yours. Neighbor is enemy. "Spirit" is a term in power. Mere resolution of a physical boundary may not be possible without a shift in spirit. Tolerating a contraction of boundary requires a leap of outlook. Definition of boundary requires a contraction that only broader spirit can encompass.

Yes, candies and carrots play a role. Parties to resolutions must get something: it must benefit mutual self-interest (everyone agrees). Those involved must feel submission to a boundary (constriction) is worth something, some expansion (economic, self-worth, opportunities of various sorts). But another sort of change is necessary too — in the realm Blake calls Vision, Imagination, Poetic Genius. Shifts in mental *and* physical boundaries feed and tug at each other in dumbfounding ways.

What does one do with the emotional knot or core that is compressed pain, ecstasy, hate, domination, submission, caring, sex, hunger, fear, worry, grief, madness and the drive for truth?

All of these fuse in a dense navel, congealed ball, fist. The knot can be radioactive, malignant, demonic, longing, aching for the freedom of good moments, hoping against hope it won't stuff good moments with rot.

I've rarely seen a tiger or lion without experiencing a glow emanating from its body. I've seen the same glow in whales. Is it a body bliss? A bliss deeper than body that glows through body?

We look at complex systems of domination and cooperation in animals. Dominance hierarchies can be a form of cooperation. Sly use of cooperation can be a form of domination. There are many moments of just-so-ness. Grooming. Babies playing. Baby and mother in the glow, the halo. Aliveness feeling alive.

Aliveness glows.

We speak of the complex interplay of competition-cooperation — the dual strain (fury-love, heaven-hell, severity-compassion, etc.) — our conceptual tools are poor indeed. We break reality into twos. To a point, it works. What an impoverishment! But we must work with tools we find or fashion.

Sometimes we try to give the glow its due. We speak of halos, energy fields, God, emptiness, angels, circles of love. We discover poetry, mystical language, outbursts from depths, welling up of feeling, perceptual awe. We try to honor the glow, explore it, test it, learn how to relate to it, work with it. The glow is more real than money.

Can cruelty glow? Poison glow?

Blake's tiger burning bright, tiger's fearful symmetry: "Did he who made the lamb make thee?"

Tiger glows, lamb glows — cruel radiance, joy radiance.

We are attracted to what glows.

We like watching light.

Einstein: "The most beautiful experience we can have is the mysterious. It is the fundamental emotion that stands at the cradle of true art and true science."

The fact of cruelty does not cancel beauty, sometimes intensifies the latter, makes beauty all the more important.

Keats: "A thing of beauty is a joy forever."

Einstein and Keats aren't alone. Does the fact that we injure each other cancel joy?

Sometimes.

Why is evil part of the sea of beauty, the mysterious? Why is evil part of ecstasy?

Most of the time we do not know what evil is. Bliss surrounds, upholds it. Evil — whatever it is — grows out of and thrives in the same porridge as everything else. We live in the porridge. Sometimes evil goes too far and we say, "*That* is evil." By that time, the obtrusion is hard to miss. We can scarcely call it anything else. Something extreme has happened. Destruction passes a threshold. Most of the time we live with it as part of the brew, make the most of it.

If evil disappears, we disappear?

The glow covers a lot of sins.

Visionary glow gets blasted when reality hits. Visionary glow uplifts reality, if it withstands it. Visionary glow obscures reality. The glow of tigers may absorb the glow of many lambs.

Little dips into the mysterious go a long way.

Bits of science, bits of art, bits of myth and mystical awe keep us going. Making a living is part of the clearing in the jungle needed to support this. To reverse the order kills soul. How much soul murder is possible before disappearing is one experiment in process. The Bible warns against hypertrophy of economics: don't live by bread alone, the letter kills, spirit gives life. Will money be the black hole that swallows us? Money in the service of awe or awe in the service of money? What mystical root is awe of money tapping?

Sample and compare truths:

"Power is the best aphrodisiac."

"The most beautiful experience we can have is the mysterious."

We are defined by our worst moments, not our best.

We are defined by our best moments, not our worst.

It is sometimes helpful to imagine the entire Bible is a story about one person, you or me. Something like the movie *Groundhog Day*, although infinitely more telling. In *Groundhog Day*, the protagonist keeps repeating the same day until he gets it right. The Bible is something like that, but far more complicated.

Imagine the entire Bible is a magnification-minification of a micromoment of soul, a glimpse of soul structure, a soul instant stretched into narratives.

God's voice, our many voices, love, hate, sexual and social conquest, ambition, power, justice, mercy, annihilation, catastrophe, faith, caring, loyalty, deprivation, awe, guilt, fear, terror, wrath, fury, misery, loss, prophecy and dreams, realism, attraction and repulsion, virtues and failings, strengths and weaknesses, favorites, miracles, backsliding: a drama rotating around apprehension of who we are, what life is, what

God wants, what we want, what is possible and impossible, what happens and fails to happen. A door left open, another chance.

Does something always poison new beginnings? When we open the door for Elijah at the Passover Seder, not many of us can say the words in the Haggadah attached to this opening. They curse our enemies. Not many of us can mobilize the full force of bitterness needed to curse anyone wholeheartedly, let alone multitudes. So we reinterpret such utterances to be about the evil inclination. We hope Elijah's spirit will help us curb, sublimate, reshape the evil in us all. A universalizing rather than parochializing tendency.

Blake did the same with Psalms of David. The enemies David asks God to wipe out refer to destructive forces of self, rightly represented as multitudes. Blake sees the Bible as a manifestation of Poetic Genius, Vision, Imagination. Every literal action and person depicted becomes an emblem of a tendency or movement of spirit, delineation of motive forces, tendencies, the astounding play of crosscurrents of self or soul or spirit or psyche. Everything we are made of.

The Bible codes competing tendencies, all of which are real — ghastly, ennobling, and mysterious interplays of cruelty and kindness, tribal and individual battles, wrestling with each other and wrestling with what is beyond reach. Never-ending story, par excellence. I fear we can learn more about human nature and problems we face from any page of the Bible than from any day at the United Nations or in Congress, or on visits to the local mall. We may find momentary solutions to get us from day to day, pastework, but unless problems set in the Bible are met, "solutions" slip into regrets.

Odd message: unless justice and mercy take hold, our work will be destructive. But there is much in us working against the realization of such a message being possible or realistic or justifiable. The Bible does not resolve this bind. It notes it. It leaves things open somewhat.

All sorts of hordes, massacres, cataclysms, annihilations, salvific moments, peaks, strivings, yearnings, losses, regroupings go on in us much of the time. They are our feelings, states of being, tendencies, "neonic" actions. Annihilating irruptions of wrath work in subtle ways throughout the day. Sometimes not so subtly. Overwhelming surges of love do too. Practical skills feed all manner of motives and endeavors, good and ill.

Freud associated number (lots of something in a dream) with emotional intensity. More = greater intensity. I don't know any extended work or collection of works as emotionally intense as the biblical voice(s). Shakespeare is second.

I don't doubt today we need something more or other than biblical reality. But not less. If we fail to face or incorporate what the Bible deals with, we will not find psychic or social or cultural or spiritual muscle and flexibility to work with what our day demands.

What does it mean to truly flourish, to be successful?

What does it mean to be a human being?

My bias, prejudice, vision, affirmation, witness, my Reality:

Let us picture a vast sea or atmosphere of ecstasy. It bathes our skin, soaks our souls, our spirits breathe it. It permeates body. One moment it is our body. One moment it sweeps body up, dissolves body, swells, floods, uplifts. You do not pin it down.

There are moments of spirit when you don't know where you are — who you are, you don't care, it's so wonderful, moments of grace. You are grateful it happens. It provides reference points for life, a sense of freedom.

It can happen anywhere, anytime. Early morning, going to bed, with a lover, alone in the country, on the cross, in the subway, after a therapy session, reading Plato or Joyce, kayaking with your child, starving to death.

When it is happening you are usually harmless. That is part of its goodness. For moments, you can feel good without doing harm. For moments, you can be ecstatic at no one's expense.

You may or may not include the other in your ecstasy. In the latter case, a problem ensues, since you likely are out of contact with the place of the other when you are placeless. You do not know where the other really is, and when the other bristles at your incomprehension, you are stung.

In one or another form, better or worse, there are seas of pain and seas of ecstasy. Atmospheres of pain. Pain everywhere, sometimes localizeable.

Picture the two as alternate, separate worlds, sometimes oscillating, reversing.

Picture the two superimposed on each other so that you live in two worlds, breathe in two atmospheres at once. Something like having two eyes and a single field of vision. Sometimes the superimpositions are somewhat visible, sometimes relatively seamless.

Picture the two whipped together in a mixmaster, ingredients contributing a new taste, a new brew. Hints or traces of original elements remain.

Seas of ecstasy and pain, separating, fusing everywhichway.

There are better and worse ecstasies, better and worse pains. Sickly ecstasies, healthy pains. A good pain is better than a bad ecstasy. Every combination and relative separation of good-bad ecstasy/pain is possible.

At times it seems as if free-floating beatific-horrific states compete for psychosocial runway space to land on. Free floating ecstasy looks for events to soak into. Free-floating terror and pain do too. Combinations of ecstasy and horror can be bloodcurdling or ennobling. Ecstatic-horrific thrills can enter any combination of so-called positive and/or negative states or happenings. I think we have a perverse need to taste all combinations imaginable, and then some. It is part of curiosity and wonder. We are lucky if we do this without causing grave injury.

To our credit, we seek safe channels for permutations of imaginative adventure—plays, shows, religious experiences, art. But we don't live in bottles. We shape events in the image of our affective preoccupations. In one portion of reality, a saint, in another a body blown to pieces, in another a movie or book, a law, garbage thrown out and collected, mystical moments making life whole, depressing struggles wasting and organizing experience, work giving one something to do.

Dead or numb periods. Nothing happening. Boredom or restlessness, nervous emptiness.

Everydayness, just plain me, hanging out, taking it easy, playing like a child, earnest, driven, searching, waiting. Unexpectedly something happens and I'm swept into something interesting.

When you least expect it, when your guard is down—beatific moments, grace moments. They take you by surprise, sweep you off your feet like love. No one needs to be there. It just happens. It just happens because you couldn't help but let aliveness be alive. Disarming aliveness. You are surprised by what aliveness can be.

It is my absolute conviction that such happy moments are better than the sickly thrill of blowing up a child or dismembering a potential lover picked up in a bar or making a stock market kill. I avow ecstatic currents run through these. I avow the mad, dumbfounding, and often useful circuit connecting, intertwining beatific-horrific ecstasies and beatific-horrific agonies (on the order of an emotional corpus callosum connecting areas of experiencing).

I avow the beauty and value of beatific moments when one is doing nothing and there's nothing to do, when action is part of play, when one doesn't lift a finger and goes on experiencing and experiencing, until fading, lingering begins.

It is a crazy world, and people do kill themselves because they aren't in the stock market when it goes up and their friends make money. The ecstasy of being alive is not always enough to sustain a life overly warped by economic comparisons. The ecstasy of being alive is scant consolation for those who fail.

But I avow the ecstasy of being alive is the core of our existence, and one way or another we do best when we bite off a bit of it and work to make it something we can share, work to make it something that another reverberates to, work to make it something that makes life better — whether an invention that eases living, a new medication or medical procedure, a genuinely creative legal process or idea, a book, a smile, a good word or touch, an insightful comment that brightens the day.

My father, at a time when the sleaziness of law and business sickened him, saw a man tending a railroad gate at a country crossing. The man's face cut my father to the core. He felt the face simple, weathered, free, revealing a natural rhythm, pace, wisdom — just so. My father felt this man was himself, the real him, the him he was meant to be, the core self. Whether he saw an angel at the crossing, a projection, an idealization — my father was transfigured by the moment and returned to his law practice with a new devotion, a renewed spirit. We do not know if this man was mean and cruel, if he beat his children, if he really was Elijah disguised, or if he was an ordinary guy, both nice and nasty. He played a releasing role, a kind of spontaneous psychospiritual chiropractory. Soul setting. Reshaping each other's relationship to the sea of ecstasy, filtering the latter through a good place in the heart, a place where we touch each other — we do this for each other on a daily basis, in many ways. It is part of what makes life most worthwhile.

And what of creative horror? A source of our fascination with Oedipus is that we know he will be horrified with himself as his journey of consciousness unfolds. Tragedy often has a horrific moment of recognition. How can I have done this, how can this be me or part of my being, my reality? How can life be this way, how can this be so! Tragedy moves toward a moment of horrific self-recognition. One recognizes a reality one did not think possible, one hoped could not be possible. Tragedy rubs our noses in what we would wish out of existence. We see ourselves in the mirror of events and gasp.

There is a feeling that what we do will turn out well. We will not get killed or maimed in battle. We will live a decent life. If we rise to the top, we will govern well. Our books will be read. People will shake our hands, welcome us. We will study, improve, be good natured, appreciated. In tragedy, fairy tale endings bite the dust. What is revealed about the state of things, ourselves, life is the unbearable, the ghastly. What is revealed is something deeply true.

Horrific self-recognition implies a frame of reference wider than myself, a reference point beyond what I have done or may do. Even in suicide there is a glimpse of a greater horizon being narrowed. Horrific self-recognition implies a wound to goodness I did not think possible. It is precisely an underlying sense of goodness that makes tragic horror acute.

The sense that life is not supposed to be this way reaches new levels. It goes beyond the cynical, sentimental "but life's not fair." It works in realms beyond naiveté without totally letting go of innocence. It teaches that wherever we are, whatever level we have reached, there is another possibility at work that may soon meet us, a maddening revelation whose stare will soon catch us. Tragedy teaches us about the flaw in goodness, but it is because goodness is a real presence in life — a real aspiration, a profound value — that flaws count.

Tragedy connects us with the excluded, sets bones of self in joints. It cuts through surface selves necessary for living and brings into view structures we overlook to get through a day. It would be difficult to make a living if one stared all day at tragic truths. Tragic literature does the work for us, while we go on our way. Oddly, the truths disclosed on stage prophesy with cunning accuracy what whispers between the bones of our lives and, at times, blossoms into nightmarish happenings we'd give anything to avoid.

"If I knew then, what I know now" is almost beside the point. Now is another then: the process goes on. A sense of reconciliation, at-onement with oneself, is positive, a contribution to getting along with the kind of person one learns one is. But a portion of reconciliation is always premature, a rest before another running start. Soon enough, tectonic plates shift and one is shaking, falling through unimaginable openings, states one prayed would never find one.

At times, there is nothing one can do with the places that swallow one. One just tries to get through what's happening, an equivalent of hiding in bed, pulling the covers over one's head, waiting for it to pass. The best one can do is endure, hope the weather changes.

Not all horror brings us to self-recognition, not immediately, per-haps not ever. Freud wrote that part of the death drive is lost, like a product of entropy — a bit of energy disappears, rather than transforms. A soldier may never fully recover from the kinds of death he sees. A man may partly die and go on living. The Holocaust creates a hole, a crater in history, in self. If tragedy is irrelevant now, it is because it cannot teach us more. Perhaps comedy and dumb violence is in, because we have given up on processing or making sense of what underlies the tragic. Horror paralyzes us. Psychospiritual metabolism is jammed.

Nevertheless, tragic work has a lot to teach us, a lot to do. It nibbles on the edges of monstrosity, here and there piercing the heart. Tragedy is in a state of shock but will come back. One of the most hideous tragedies of all is what we will be like if it does not.

Tragedy mimics birth on a psychic level. What is born is agonizing truths, dreaded gestures and happenings, grotesque twists in being. Recognition sweeps death up with it, as death becomes part of an-guished birth, and birth ecstasy encompasses pain.

Horror fascinates us. It scares us into the realization that we can never fathom the complexities of the forces we are enmeshed in. We can be wiped out, warped, embalmed at any moment in any number of ways. Tragedy tries to channel what it can of complexities we can never master. It sifts filaments of destructive horror through a kind of parallel world of creative horror, where self-recognition and renewal have some breathing room.

In tragedy one measures self against the full complexity of forces portrayed. Simple ways out, shallow escape routes, are cut off. For the moment, we approach, wincing and shuddering, the immensity that challenges us.

Let us give religious imagination its due. For example, the idea of God as a perfect unity who encompasses and fills all worlds. There is no place outside God. No place or placelessness.

This includes the Holocaust, racial cleansing of every sort, mass starvation and oppression in Africa, terrorist bombings maiming innocents in subways. This must include other kinds of starvation and terrorism, the thrilling embalming fluid of the stock market, mass-marketed economic depravity, political posturing that twists lives out of shape.

Wherever I go, You are. I find You through my deadness, my numbness, in the depths of my madness. Yes, of course, You are in the sky, clouds, stars, light, dark, the good things in life. But You are also in the monsters of the deep. You are in my pain when I hurt my child, my wife, my sister. You are the pain of the Other. You are in my joy. You are the joy of the Other. You are the black hole in me, the radiance in me. You are my failure, my success. Wherever I run, like Jonah, there You are. I try to throw You off, but You teach me life is precious. You open my heart with love. When I am tired of life, You are there.

Numberless horrors and holies: none escape You.

There is really not much to say if God is in every horror, every minute particular of evil. We might as well lay down and die.

A callow, jejune, and garish consideration: taking ourselves out (impossible?) implies we feel exempt from horror and evil, or ought to be exempt. Bad stuff ought not be us, part of us, afflict us. Basic resentment, indignation: why are we not what we imagine God to be? How can we live with ourselves and God if we meet God in every contingency, every drop of alienation, every bit of wrath.

Because there is no respite or reprieve in God, God built in a Sabbath point of soul, a shalom center. It is there for everyone at all times in the turbulence, in the dead sea.

"From my flesh I see God."

Do I see You in poisoned ecology? Are You in pollution in the places You shine most brightly? In the radiation of Hiroshima, in the chemicals and oils suffocating the ocean, sea monsters not invented when scribes wrote high-low adventures with You? Do You glisten in the countless misunderstandings we wound each other with each day?

Where are You in the mean death of children? Always with us?

The whole world is filled with Your Glory?

Some say variable good-evil is God speaking in different languages to different people.

Much callowness clusters around God. Is God in the callowness?

All the worlds are filled with Your Glory? You are the Glory in all the worlds?

The bitterness in a mother's heart over a child lost is not wiped out by joys she feels for her other children.

God wipes us out with horrors, with love. Uplifts us through horrors, through love.

And what about moments of opening, good moments, good times? In psychoanalysis a patient may bring in a good dream, have a good session. These are dreams or sessions that enable an individual to feel life's goodness. It is good to be alive. These are moments that enable love of life, moments of grace, freedom. They come from hard work, staying with ghastly things, staying close to one's own sin, one's own pain. Finally, opening.

One hopes to continue opening.

Sometimes I think opening is a little like learning to ride a bike or typewriting. Once you get the feel, you can do it again, more easily, often. For many people, it's a "feel" not gotten easily, the capacity for good moments marred early. Perhaps for many the movement toward opening is a purely secular business. For me, there is a touch of the sacred in it. Perhaps more than a touch.

Mystical vision depicts many kinds, degrees, phases of love. Sometimes divine love takes the form of a marriage bond, heart to heart, mouth to mouth. Ineffable nearness. A perfect bond.

Sometimes the light of love "may shine forth with its intense heat, its intense light, like a burning fire." A consciousness of the heart *and* mind, a self-nullifying surrender of soul and body to God. The more zeroing of self, the more "room" for light and fire.

With all one's heart and all one's soul and all one's might.

Body is not left behind. Body is eternal delight. The yumminess of body fills with divine light.

Life of life. Light of light.

God's light in a lover's face. I think back over my life, difficulties in loving. Every love brought me closer to heaven.

Body love comes with me. Touch is a taste of heaven — touch comes with me. It liquefies into other streams of light. Body sensations fill with light. You roll a ball of snow down a hill and it keeps growing. Sensation lights, feeling lights, ecstatic thought lights roll together, parts of light through everything, everything part of light's momentum.

Pleasures lap into one another. Joys flow into each other. Ecstasies summate.

As if a trainman throws a switch in the tracks and direction changes. Where does love of God come from? Is it in sensuous love? Parent-child caring? How does it happen that one day one sees stars, feels a breeze, clouds open and one's soul touches God?

One of my sons shows me what he calls, "The Phenomenon." We swim across part of a lake to a place where we see light ripples on tree leaves ever changing, gentle, light fingertips, halos vibrating. A little area where trees are alive with quivering light, liquefied stars sparkling in shimmering leaves. It is, of course, sunlight reflected by the water. I do not know if my son sees God in this, but he feels the thrill of mystery, the amazement beauty brings.

Pleasure, joy, ecstasy commingle as we go along. At some point, perhaps from the outset unconsciously or semiconsciously, ecstatic love takes on a life of its own, eventually bypassing itself. Ecstatic love can be like a catapult that rockets love past ecstasy. Ecstatic love is a gift that opens possibilities beyond itself.

Enjoyment is a crude term for the light that kindles soul with fire, intense and sweet. The heavenward flame.

Mystics tell of "one" love that incorporates and/or dissolves and/or transcends distinctions made in all other loves. Lesser loves are steps or vehicles or parts of an even more amazing, unifying love. Other loves are tastes of the love of loves.

For myself, the Light seems to be somewhat independent of love. Love may or may not be attached to it. Also, I'm not sure surrender must play much of a role. In my life, Light just happened. I did nothing to find it. I did not even know about it beforehand. I'm not sure it made me a better person. It didn't come because I was terrific. I'm glad it became a real presence for me. I don't know what I'd have done without it. How poor and empty things might have been without it. Things are hard enough as it is.

I can think of times Light seemed to be born of pain, but this is not always so. Sometimes Light kindles Light. Sometimes Light comes out of nowhere. Sometimes it is kindled by a kiss.

Work gives meaning to life. Affectionate bonds give life meaning. Curiosity, wonder, awe, compassion. Pick your fuel. I can only confess that for myself I can't imagine any of these would mean what they mean, yield what they yield, if the Light did not inform them.

Is goodness tied to Light? One might think so. I've certainly tried to be a better person, worked hard at it. Still, I'm still me, or versions of me. Still working at it, knocking against the hard stuff. Causing pain, feeling pain. In the pits. The Light's been with me free of charge. Like birth. Or, rather—it comes for the same price Life does. It comes along with life. I can't help feeling it gives Life to life.

Is it like this for everyone? Sometimes when I talk like this, sophisticated New York colleagues look oddly at me. They are into careers, material goods, life as it is, the good life. I've not heard many say the Light is so important to them. I doubt I'm very different from them, except the Light makes everything in my life shine. The Light opens everything up to radiance. The Light makes everything seem worthwhile, whole, beautiful, astonishing.

Is it a bonus, or the meat?

"In Your light do I see light." Thrills, shivers when I think this, feel this. Indescribably beyond thrills and shivers.

Years ago — I don't remember exactly when — a phrase in a song that is part of the conclusion of every Jewish prayer service lodged in me, brought me home. It is a line in the "Aleinu," a song of praise. It is something like: "He is our God, there is none else." There is no one, nothing else. This line set off reverberations that never stop. I'm at a loss to convey it.

There is only God? Everywhere at all times? Everything everywhere is always God?

Perhaps it could mean there are no Gods but our God, as in "Hear, O Israel, the Lord is our God, the Lord is One." *Echad* (One)–*Shalom* (Peace)–*Ayin* (Nothing)–*En Sof* (Infinite). That may be, but that waters it down.

Perhaps it is more like, "I look at my sons and see God. I look at my patients and see God. I look at my wife and see God. I look at you and see God. I feel God in every fiber of being, my being."

No, it is more. It is more.

NOTES AND REFERENCES

p. vii: I heard Hanna Arendt speak on ecstasy and thinking at the New School for Social Research, New York City, in the 1960s.

p. vii: Eigen, M. (1993). *The Electrified Tightrope*. Northvale, N.J.: Jason Aronson.

———— (1998). *The Psychoanalytic Mystic*. London and New York: Free Association Books.

p. vii: Federn, P. (1957). *Ego Psychology and the Psychoses*. London: Maresfield Reprints. For additional discussion of originary, boundless I-feeling in Federn, see my book *The Psychotic Core* (1986; Northvale, N.J.: Jason Aronson), chap. 4.

p. vii: Winnicott, D. W. (1992). *The Maturational Processes and the Facilitating Environment*. New York: International Universities Press.

———— (1989). *Psycho-Analytic Explorations*. Ed. C. Winnicott, R. Shepherd, and M. Davis. Cambridge: Harvard University Press.

———— (1992). *Through Paediatrics to Psycho-Analysis: Collected Papers*. New York: Bruner Mazel.

p. vii: Milner, M. (1957). *On Not Being Able to Paint*. New York: International Universities Press, esp. the Appendix. Also, see my amplification of Milner's orgasmic symbolic experiencing in *The Electrified Tightrope*, chap. 14.

p. vii: Faith plays an increasingly important role as Bion's work unfolds — for example, in *Attention and Interpretation* (1970; Northvale, N.J.: Jason Aronson). See my interpretation of Faith in Bion in *The Electrified Tightrope* (chaps. 11 and 17), and *The Psychoanalytic Mystic* (chaps. 3–5).

p. viii–ix: Eigen, M. (1986). *The Psychotic Core*.

———— (1996). *Psychic Deadness*. Northvale, N.J.: Jason Aronson.

———— (1999). *Toxic Nourishment*. London: Karnac.

———— (2001). *Damaged Bonds*. London: Karnac.

p. 4: Freud, S. (1914). "On narcissism: an introduction." *Standard Edition*, 14:73–102.

p. 5: Reich, W. (1949). *Character Analysis*. New York: Farrar, Straus & Cudahy.

p. 7: Federn, P. (1957). *Ego Psychology and the Psychoses*.

pp. 9–11: Plotinus (1991). *The Enneads*. Trans. Stephen MacKenna; abridged by John Dillon. London and New York: Penguin Books. For quotes, see 386, 545.

p. 13: Lacan sometimes suggests that nothing is hidden by certain acts of hiding. One hides in order to feel something is hidden. In this context, something covers nothing. There is, too, the psycho-dynamic reflection that you hide in order to hide the fact that no one wants you. By hiding you can pretend someone is trying to find you. Thus, feeling hidden obscures the grisly realization that no one seeks you — a subtle but potent defense. That is, feeling hidden makes you feel wanted.

p. 14: For an elaboration of "taint" and "warp," see "Demonized Aspects of the Self" (chap. 16) in *The Electrified Tightrope* and "The Counterpart" (chap. 9) in *Psychic Deadness*.

p. 17: Lewin, B. (1973). *Selected Writings of Bertram D. Lewin*. Ed. J. A. Arlow. New York: The Psychoanalytic Quarterly.

pp. 37–38: Lacan, J. (1978). *The Four Fundamental Concepts of Psycho-Analysis*. Trans. A Sheridan. Ed. Jacques-Allain Miller. New York: Norton.

p. 37: Freud, S. (1911). "Psycho-analytic notes on an autobiographical account of a case of paranoia (demential paranoides)." *Standard Edition*, 13:1–162. See my account of Schreber's case in *The Psychotic Core*.

p. 39: Joseph Campbell used the phrase "Follow your bliss" while discussing the troubadours and chivalry, a kind of apotheosis to the birth of modern individualism ("Each knight enters the forest in a different place — finds or makes his own path in the forest.") I heard Campbell say things like this in talks many years ago. Boris loved Campbell's writings.

p. 45: Grotsein, J. S. (1981). *Splitting and Projective Identification*. Northvale, N.J.: Jason Aronson.

p. 46: Freud, S. (1940). "An outline of psycho-analysis." *Standard Edition*, 23:141–207.

p. 47: I heard Cairn say this at the New School for Social Research in the 1960s. His was a kind of Husserlian "proof" of the "immortality" of consciousness because of its temporal structure.

p. 48: For the image of explosiveness in the birth and shattering of consciousness, see W. R. Bion (1970), *Attention and Interpretation*, and Eigen (1998), *The Psychoanalytic Mystic*, chap. 3.

p. 64: "life's fitful fever," "restless ecstasy," Shakespeare's *Macbeth*; "potent and infectious fevers," Shakespeare's *Timon of Athens*.

p. 67: This "conjugation," or set of transformations, was put on the Bion internet mail list in 1998 by Dr. Eli Garfinkle, a student of Clifford Scott's. He heard Scott say things like this in talks. Dr. Garfinkle and the Bion mail list webmaster, Dr. Silvio Merciai, have given me permission to make my own use of this material. W. Clifford Scott was a creative Canadian psychoanalyst, influenced by Melanie Klein and Wilfred R. Bion, among others.

p. 71: Bion, W. R. (1980). *Bion in New York and São Paulo*. Ed. Francesca Bion. Strathclyde: Clunie Press.

pp. 73–74: Bion, W. R. (1982). *The Long Week-End, 1897–1919*. Abingdon: Fleetwood Press.

——— (1961). *Experiences in Groups*. London: Tavistock.

p. 76: "fever," "uncertain sickly appetite," "desire is death," "frantic-mad with evermore unrest," "black as hell, as dark as night," Shakespeare's Sonnet 147.

p. 77: "Within be fed . . . ," Shakespeare's Sonnet 146.

p. 78: "God, the Place." Hebrew has many names for God. Nouns can be made into names for God. In the Haggadah, the book used at the Passover Seder, God is called *Hamakom*: *Ha* = The, and *Makom* = Place.

p. 82: "Energy is Eternal delight," William Blake, *The Marriage of Heaven and Hell*.

pp. 83–84: Winnicott, D. W. (1989). *Psycho-Analytic Explorations*.

p. 85: "For everything that lives is holy," William Blake, *The Marriage of Heaven and Hell*.

p. 85: "He who sees the Infinite in all . . . ," William Blake, "There is

No Natural Religion." The remaining Blake quotes are from *The Marriage of Heaven and Hell*.

p. 87: "The most beautiful experience we can have . . . ," Albert Einstein. I got this from a poster I saw at the Liberty Science Center in Jersey City, N.J.

p. 87: "A thing of beauty . . . ," Keats, *Endymion*.

p. 88: "Power is the best aphrodisiac." I don't know where I first heard this, but we all heard Henry Kissinger say it.

p. 89: Nicholas Berdyaev uses the term "neonic" to convey the sense of birthing new or emergent life, actions that bring forth soul. He associates it with freedom, "neonic freedom," based on ever being born. Here I associate it with disruption and omnipresent change.

p. 96: "From my flesh, I see God," Job 19:26.

p. 97: "may shine forth . . . ," Rabbi Schneur Zalman of Liadi, *Likutei Amarim — Tanya*. (1984; Brooklyn, N.Y.: Kehot Publication Society).

p. 98: "In your light . . . ," Psalm 36.

About the author : MICHAEL EIGEN is a psychologist and psychoanalyst. He is Associate Clinical Professor of Psychology in the Postdoctoral Program in Psychotherapy and Psychoanalysis at New York University. His numerous books include *Damaged Bonds* (2001), *Toxic Nourishment* (1999), *The Psychoanalytic Mystic* (1998), *Psychic Deadness* (1996), and *The Psychotic Core* (1986). Eigen is also a Senior Member at the National Psychological Association for Psychoanalysis.